THE POLITICAL THEORY

OF T. H. GREEN

The Political Theory

of

T. H. Green

SELECTED WRITINGS

EDITED BY

John R. Rodman

HARVARD UNIVERSITY

New York

APPLETON-CENTURY-CROFTS

Division of Meredith Publishing Company

PRINTED IN THE UNITED STATES OF AMERICA

E-22560

CONTENTS

INTRODUCTION

GREEN AS POLITICAL THEORIST

T. H. GREEN (1836-1882) has importance for anyone interested in either politics or philosophy, and particularly for anyone concerned about the fate of Political Theory in our time.

As a reformer of practical Liberal thinking, Green laid out one of the main lines of development from the upper-class 'Nightwatchman State' of the mid-19th century to the democratic 'Welfare State' of the 20th century. His representative significance as the articulator of an advancing trend of opinion, and his influence as a mediator between two stages of political and social order, make him the most important political thinker between John Stuart Mill (1806-1873) and the present. His lecture on "Liberal Legislation and Freedom of Contract" (1881) is indispensable for understanding and appraising the new pattern of power and policy that has grown up in Britain and, to some extent, in other liberal-democratic states, superseding *laissez-faire* and rendering irrelevant the diagnosis and prescription of revolutionary Marxism—a doctrine based in part, ironically, on an analysis of British conditions.

As a reformer in philosophy, Green was instrumental in emancipating Oxford philosophy from the tutelage of theology and classical philology, and establishing it as an autonomous discipline without

1

sacrificing any of its traditional breadth of concern. His "Introductions" to Hume (1874) launched the first wave of the philosophical criticism that was to topple the Naturalistic viewpoint from its position of supremacy in British intellectual life.[1] Green's constructive work remained incomplete, partly because of his early death. But the flourishing of Idealist metaphysics, theory of knowledge, and ethics that set in so rapidly in the 1880's and ruled British philosophy into the early decades of the 20th century, would have been inconceivable without the foundations laid by Green's influential Oxford lectures, particularly the course that provided the basis of the posthumously published book, *Prolegomena to Ethics*. Finally, of all the British and American exponents of Philosophical Idealism, Green remains—along with F. H. Bradley, who had been his pupil—one of the few still worth reading today for the intrinsic quality of their thought, and not merely for their historical significance as representatives of an intellectual epoch.

Above all, Green's importance lies in the way he combined the role of philosopher with the role of political thinker, so that theoretical and practical themes were interwoven in the kind of synthesis that has perennially marked the intellectual enterprise of Political Theory. Although Green's chief work of Political Theory, the posthumously published lectures on *The Principles of Political Obligation*, cannot be placed in the first rank with Plato's *Republic*, Hobbes' *Leviathan*, or Hegel's *Philosophy of Right*, still Green is the last political theorist of anything like classic stature that we can discern from our mid-20th century standpoint. And the theory of 'positive freedom,' which Green above all others developed and

---

[1] The senses in which the terms 'Naturalism' and 'Idealism' are used here are discussed in Section II, below.

gave new applications to, remains—although clearly incomplete—the last major development in Political Theory. It is still the pivotal issue on which contemporary controversies about the relations among liberty, democracy, and the Welfare State are apt to turn.[2]

I

When Green was a young man at Balliol College, Oxford—first as an undergraduate and then as a Lecturer and Fellow of Balliol—he was uncertain whether his vocation lay in academic work, in journalism, in government work connected with education, or in the Christian ministry.[3] As things turned out, he never really left Oxford. But in committing himself to the responsibilities of academic work, he did not renounce entirely the life of practical affairs or the larger vocation of the citizen and reformer. As Tutor of Balliol in the 1870's under Jowett's Mastership, he bore (in his own words) "practically the whole subordinate management of the college,"[4] and

[2] On the historical importance of the idea of 'positive freedom,' see Guido de Ruggiero, *The History of European Liberalism* (London, 1927); Noel Annan, "Misconceptions of Freedom" (*The Listener*, Feb. 19, 1959); and David Nicholls, "Positive Liberty: 1880-1914" (*American Political Science Review*, March 1962).

Recent political writings turning on the issue of 'positive freedom' include: E. H. Carr, *The New Society* (London, 1951), and Sir Isaiah Berlin, *Two Concepts of Liberty* (Oxford, 1959). With the latter, compare: Marshall Cohen, "Berlin and the Liberal Tradition" (*Philosophical Quarterly*, July 1960).

[3] *The Works of Thomas Hill Green* (London, 1885-88), Vol. III, page xxxv. The editorship of *The Times of India* was actually offered Green in 1863.

[4] *Works*, III, lxi.

he worked to bridge the gap between the University and the modern world through scholarships for the talented poor, university education for women, and extension courses for adult workingmen. Outside the University, he was active in a multitude of special purpose groups ranging from the Reform League (for extension of the suffrage), through the National Education League (for reform in education), to the United Kingdom Alliance (for temperance legislation). From his participation in the affairs of Oxford's North Ward Liberal Association, he knew at first hand the drudgeries and the satisfactions of party politics at the ward and town levels. As an elected member of the town School Board and the town Council, he also knew something of the responsibilities of political office. He did not spare himself when friends standing for Parliament required his services as a speaker; and he was himself urged to stand for Parliament, but declined for personal reasons—mainly his failing health and his desire for time to prepare his lectures on ethics for publication.

In the last analysis, it was more as a don than as a politician that Green had his effect upon British politics. He was too reserved to be a 'great personality' in the usual sense, too scrupulous to preach a doctrine to disciples, and too much inclined to complication and qualification to be a popular lecturer. But his combination of intellectual honesty, moral earnestness, and concern for the problems of practical life made a remarkable impact on the contemporaries who knew him and, above all, on the Oxford undergraduates—the future statesmen, teachers, and churchmen—who went forth inspired to change society, or at least prepared to acquiesce in the justice of its being changed. Some impression of his impact on this elite and, through it, on the broader public can be gained from many a late-Victorian and Edwardian memoir, as well as from the popular novel by Mrs. Humphry Ward, *Robert Elsmere* (1888), in which Green appears as 'Mr. Henry Grey,' the donnish inspirer of true reformers of the world.

Above all, it was the 'condition of the people' issue that had Green's attention. He was one of those perceptive men who realized that British Liberalism, with its elitist and *laissez-faire* traditions, faced a crisis with the emergence of an urban and rural working class, which—propertyless, hindered by law from effective organization, and virtually excluded from participation in the political system—was left so dependent on the capitalists, the landowners, and the vagaries of the trade cycle, that its condition made a mockery of the ideals that Liberals professed. The optimistic assumption that the uninhibited pursuit of individual profit automatically worked out to the common good of all had come up against the hard facts of life in the 19th century. The appalling facts about the long hours and low wages, the insecure, unhealthy, and degrading conditions of work, the chronic drunkenness in which relief from misery was sought, and the sordid living conditions that had to be suffered by the men, women, and children of the urban proletariat had been documented in the evidence gathered by such bodies as the Sadler Committee as early as 1832.[5] The irony was that these conditions were the product of the same Industrial Revolution that created unprecedented wealth. An even more savage irony lay in the fact that this system of dependence and oppression had grown up under the aegis of the Liberal ideal of freedom, articulated in

[5] *Report of the Committee on the Bill to Regulate the Labour of Children in the Mills and Factories of the United Kingdom* (*Parliamentary Papers,* 1831-32, Vol. XV).

such slogans as 'free competition,' 'freedom of contract,' and 'freedom from state interference.' Considering the vast inequalities of social and political power that existed, as well as the pressure of population upon the supply of jobs and land, Green was clear that the 'freedom' of "a starving laborer to bargain for good wages with a master who offers him work" or of "the peasant farmer . . . to contract with his landlord" was more a sham 'freedom' than a real one.[6]

Green's response to this dilemma posed by the Industrial and Agricultural Revolution was threefold. First of all, he gave ardent support to measures like the Reform Bill of 1867 and the Corrupt Practices Bill of 1882—measures designed to extend the Parliamentary franchise and to eliminate the influence of wealth in the form of bribery, in short, measures designed to democratize the political system. Green's objectives were two. On the one hand, he trusted that the admission of the lower classes into participation in the political system would ensure that their interests were taken into account in legislation. In this way, class antagonism would diminish and, along with it that hostility to the positive use of governmental authority that had been natural enough in an age when a privileged few had held the reins of power. On the other hand, Green was concerned to make more widely available the opportunity for individual self-development through participation in the responsibilities of active citizenship. He was convinced that "citizenship only makes the moral man; . . . citizenship only gives that self-respect,

[6] See below, page 67. Cf. the Sadler Report: A father, asked why he permitted his children to work in such conditions, replied simply, "Necessity compels a man that has children to let them work." (Testimony of Joshua Drake.)

which is the true basis of respect for others, and without which there is no lasting social order or true morality." [7]

The second part of Green's response to the social-political dilemma of Victorian Britain consisted of various proposals for the extension and "reconstruction" of education. The reform of education was not the harmless panacea that it might appear. Although England in the 19th century fostered an educated elite, she lagged far behind countries like Germany, France, and the United States in providing elementary and secondary public education, not to mention university education for more than a privileged few. Even with the gradual spread of public education following the Education Act of 1870 and later Acts, the highly stratified character of the educational system as a whole remained a major factor in perpetuating the hierarchical class structure that has given British political democracy its peculiarly deferential style. Green's proposals all related, in one way or another, to the creation of a system of comparable educational opportunities for all, regardless of birth, wealth, or religion. His objectives in this paralleled the objectives of his support for political democracy. On the one hand, he hoped to create a more "socially united" people in place of a population "divided into the educated few and the uneducated many" and corrupted by "unconscious social insolence" and "social jealousy." On the other hand, by bringing "the sort of education which alone makes the gentleman in any true sense . . . within the reach of all," he hoped to secure every person a better opportunity to make "the best of himself." [8]   It was perhaps a utopian program; it re-

[7] *Works,* III, cxii, cxix. *Principles of Political Obligation,* §122.
[8] *Works,* III, 387-476, xlv-lviii, cxiii-cxv.

mains today unfinished business on the agenda of the Labour Party.

The third part of Green's response consisted of his support for the greater use of the state's regulatory authority in order to protect the dependent classes from exploitation. As a student of Aristotle, as well as an observer of modern town life, Green was aware that the full development of human potentialities and the life of 'excellence' presupposed a certain minimal level of material well-being and leisure. Private charity, the formation of trade unions and 'friendly societies' among the workers, and exhortations to temperance: all these modes of ameliorating 'the condition of the people' had Green's support; but he was under no illusion that they could by themselves deal with the problem. "This is an evil," he declared, "which no individual benevolence can cure. Ten thousand soup-kitchens are unavailing against it. It can only be cured by . . . legislation. . . ." [9] In his lecture on "Liberal Legislation and Freedom of Contract" (1881) Green outlined the sort of legislation he had in mind: Factory Acts regulating hours and conditions of work, Public Health Acts affecting housing, Education Acts, temperance legislation (stricter licensing, local option, etc.), and measures designed to give security of tenure to tenant farmers and to disperse land ownership. Some of these (such as the Factory Acts) Green could take for granted, though hoping for their further perfection. Others (like the Irish Land Bill) were on the verge of enactment. A few never came to pass, at least in the form Green advocated. More important than the specific measures, however, was the general pattern of 'liberal legislation' that Green sketched. And most important of all was the principle of 'positive freedom' that he introduced in

[9] *Works*, III, cxii.

order to link the various types of 'liberal legislation' as so many complementary ways of removing obstacles to the active power of men for self-development.

Green's approach to social and political issues fell primarily within the tradition of the 'Radical' wing of British Liberalism. Radicalism—the tradition of 'the more advanced reformers'—had had a relatively continuous history since agitation began in the 1770's for more equal Parliamentary representation. Particularly since the depression following the Napoleonic wars, Radicals had also agitated for the alleviation of popular economic distress; but most of them had assumed that this could be achieved simply by 'negative' legislation—that is, by Acts removing restrictions on individual behavior, and by Acts repealing the privileged status traditionally enjoyed by certain parts of the population, mainly the aristocracy and the landed gentry. Green stood squarely in the mainstream of the Radical tradition, in that almost all his practical criticisms and proposals could be subsumed under the central Radical demand for the abolition of political, social, economic, and ecclesiastical 'privilege,' and the establishment of equality of opportunity. But, as the Industrial Revolution had advanced, a cleavage had opened up within the ranks of the Radicals. Men of the older generation like John Bright and Richard Cobden, who had worked for the repeal of the Corn Laws and the extension of the franchise, tended to think these reforms sufficient and balked at the growing trend towards positive regulation of the relations between capitalist and worker, landowner and tenant. It was the nub of Green's effort to win the other Radicals, the Liberal Party as a whole, and as much of the public as possible, for the more 'positive' or 'collectivist' version of Liberal Radicalism. After Green's death, the fortunes of the cause for which he had fought were reflected in the advance from the dissenting "Radical Programme" (1885) of Joseph Chamberlain, through the "Newcastle Programme" adopted by the National Liberal Federation in 1891, to the actual legislative program of the Liberal Government of 1906.

When reformers like Green were charged with advocating revolutionary policies, they were apt to reply that their critics were the real revolutionaries. The very notion of 'The Industrial and Agricultural *Revolution*' was a Radical invention that served to emphasize that the *status quo* had first been upset by the capitalists and landowners who transformed the economic system and, in the process, turned a more or less independent peasantry into a mass of dependent laborers.[10] Radicals could then represent themselves as striving to *restore* the independence of the common man. "They say that he [Bright] is a revolutionist," exclaimed Green, "when they themselves advocate a system which empties the country of its yeomen, the natural support of true conservatism, and by treating five-sixths of the people as political aliens, leads, by inexorable necessity, to revolution." [11] The existing system, that is, would lead to revolution *if persisted in:* Green's faith in the capacity of the Liberal state to save itself by transforming itself stood in sharp contrast to Marx's doctrine of the inevitable necessity of violent revolution. Like the Fabian Socialists, Green believed in peaceful, gradual change, and he brought forth his proposals not as revolutionary demands or utopian visions, but as projections of tendencies already implicit in British development. Yet, unlike

---

[10] See Arnold Toynbee, *Lectures on the Industrial Revolution* (London, 1884). Toynbee (1852-82) was a pupil and junior colleague of Green's at Balliol.

[11] *Works,* III, cxii.

both Marx and the Fabians, he based his proposals on an explicit appeal to the moral ideal of self-realization, and he never gave the impression of relying on assertions about the supposedly categorically inevitable course of history. The idea of 'progress' was for Green, as it had been for Kant, a regulative idea for making our history intelligible to ourselves, as well as a postulate to be validated through practical action. It was not a dogma from which one could derive standards of right and wrong.

Further, Green differed from socialists of all kinds (Marxian, Fabian, Christian, and Utopian) by virtue of the limited character of his 'collectivism.' His notion of a 'common good' was limited by his axiomatic assumption that value resided ultimately in the self-development of the individual personality. Accordingly, the role of the state was limited to guaranteeing the material conditions for, and removing whenever possible the obstacles to, the life of moral self-development. If Green interpreted this formula to justify a greater role for state action than had been called for by previous Liberal theory, he was still no advocate of a full-fledged state socialism whose paternalism would leave little sphere for voluntary action. In areas where individual and group initiatives could cope, the presumption was against state interference. Finally, Green differed from socialists by virtue of his attitude towards private property. Though willing to regulate the uses made of property when they impinged upon the common good, he would have used the authority of Parliament not to nationalize the ownership of land or industry, but rather to secure for the workers of the land "some real interest in the soil" and to spread the ownership of land by removing legal sanction from primogeniture and entailment.

Green stood for an ideal that is at least nominally expressed by a present-day Conservative Party slogan:
'a property-owning democracy.' / COMMODITY OWNING /

Green's outlook did not lack conservative strands.
He was quick to appreciate the value of certain traditional institutions (such as private property, family
life, local government, the state) as media for the active self-realization of men. He was nostalgic for
the pre-industrial age of the yeoman farmer. And he
commended Burke's "true philosophic insight" that an
individual could not be understood in abstraction
from "the relations embodied in habitudes and institutions which make him what he is"—a perspective expressed negatively in Green's critique of the Lockean
idea of 'natural rights' originating in an allegedly pre-
social 'state of nature.' [12] But Green was separated
from the Conservative Party of his day (and from
the conservative or Whig wing of the Liberal Party)
by virtue of his program for reforming away traditional privilege. And he was separated from the progressive element in the Conservative Party—the 'Tory
Radicalism' and 'Tory Democracy' of the Disraelians
—by three things: a moral disapproval of the oppor-
tunistic motives of these 'aristocratic democrats;' a
hostility towards the policy of imperialism, which
seemed not only objectionable in itself but calculated
to distract attention from domestic problems; and a
rejection of the distinctive style of Tory Democracy—
government for the people, by 'the natural leaders of
society.' Green's image of democratic man was not
the deferential subject but the active, self-governing
citizen. His sworn enemy was the degrading "flunk-
eyism which pervades English society from the top to

[12] *Works*, III, 116f. *Principles of Political Obligation*, §§51ff.,
§99, and passim.

the bottom, and is incompatible with any healthy political life." [13]

This vision of the citizen, which lay at the heart of Green's politics, had two aspects. On the one hand, it was a vision of the autonomous, self-governing individual—the independent yeoman that Green had known in his early days in Yorkshire—who was no man's lackey. On the other hand, it was not a vision of uninhibited, egoistic individualism, but rather of self-restraint and concern for others within the framework of a common good shared by members of a community—a vision exemplified perhaps by the 17th-century Puritans Green so admired. The duality of this total vision of the citizen was reflected in Green's critique of contemporary life: sometimes he deplored class antagonism and social disunity; at other times he waxed indignant at the oppression and exploitation of some men by others. Similarly, the corrective emphases that Green asserted took now the form of stressing the right of the community, the common good, or the public interest over the right of individuals to use their property as they pleased, and took now the form of an envisaged liberation, e.g., "the removal of all obstructions which the law can remove to the free development of English citizens." [14] It is possible to criticize Green for not having clearly made up his mind between individualism and collectivism, between freedom and community. It would be profounder to say that he had a firm grasp of the two complementary, and often antagonistic, spiritual needs—freedom as independence, and freedom as participation in community—that men attempt to satisfy in their social-political life. He was acutely aware of the pressing need for a new form of community to heal

[13] *Works,* III, cxi.
[14] *Works,* III, cxx.

the wounds of a society whose creed of competitive individualism had licensed the exploitation of the economically weak by the economically strong in the name of 'freedom.' But he was wise enough not to flee to the other extreme and abandon the ideal of individual freedom altogether. Rather he undertook, for reasons both strategic and philosophical, to formulate the corrective primarily in terms of 'freedom' itself, and to transform Liberalism from within.

When A. V. Dicey attempted, some two decades after Green's death, to analyze the 'collectivist' pattern of policy that had succeeded the Liberal 'individualism' of the mid-19th century, he was unable to name a thinker or a doctrine that could represent the 'collectivist' stage in the way that Jeremy Bentham and 'Benthamism' had symbolized (for Dicey, at least) the 'individualist' stage.[15] From our perspective in time, it is apparent that a number of different strands of thought mediated the transition from *laissez-faire* Liberalism to the democratic Welfare State, and that not all of them were wholly 'collectivist' in character. In particular, a large part of the operative theory of the democratic Welfare State was built up by latter-day Liberal Radicals such as Green, Keynes, and Beveridge. And the actual construction of the Welfare State in practice owed much to the Liberal Governments between 1906 and World War I, which were presided over for the most part by Prime Minister Asquith, a Balliol man who had studied under Green and who subscribed to the theory of 'positive freedom.'[16]

In the view of Asquith's friend and colleague, R. B.

[15] A. V. Dicey, *Lectures on the Relation Between Law and Public Opinion* (London, 1905).

[16] See: The Earl of Oxford and Asquith, *Memories and Reflections* (Boston, 1928), Vol. I, 21ff; also Asquith's "Introduction" to Herbert Samuel's *Liberalism* (London, 1902), ix-x.

Haldane, the eventual decline of the Liberal Party in the 1920's stemmed in effect from the Liberals' not having taken even more seriously the direction pointed by Green:

We Liberals failed to realize in the beginning of 1906 that the spirit was rapidly changing, and that the outlook of Victorian Liberalism was not sufficient for the progressive movement which had set in early in the twentieth century. . . . What was needed was a new and enlightened attitude towards social problems, and this in the main we failed to adopt. . . . [Among other signs of the times,] The teaching of men like Thomas Hill Green was penetrating deeply, and that turned on more than *laissez-faire*. There was an earnestness about State Intervention to be seen everywhere.[17]

To see the teaching of Green in terms of 'State Intervention' was, of course, to see it somewhat one-sidedly; Haldane wrote from the perspective of a Liberal who had moved on to the Labour Party. There is a sense in which the Liberal Party declined because it took the teaching of Green—with all its balanced ambivalence between individualism and collectivism —very seriously indeed, and so was outbid in a more collectivist age. But the teaching of Green had long since passed beyond the bounds of the Liberal Party and had helped form the intellectual atmosphere that Socialists and Conservatives breathed. If the effect of Green's teaching on Liberals was to make them aware of the need for 'State Intervention,' its effect

[17] R. B. Haldane (Viscount Haldane), *An Autobiography* (Garden City, 1929), 228f. Haldane served as Secretray of State for War (1905-1912) and as Lord Chancellor (1912-15 and 1924). One of the few non-academic philosophers of the Idealist movement and an ardent Hegelian (see his *The Pathway to Reality*), he had been led to the study of Hegel partly by the writings of Green (*Autobiography*, 8, 21).

on Socialists and Conservatives was to remind them that the ultimate end justifying the use of state authority was the maintenance of conditions in which individual self-realization was possible. The teaching of Green thus cut two ways, depending upon the context; and the ambivalence of Green has been built into the very pattern of policy that comprises the 20th-century Welfare State. In this perspective, it seems no great exaggeration to say with Laski (in 1940) that it was "Under the philosophic auspices of Green . . . [that] the main gains in the legislation of the last fifty years are to be recorded. The gains were great, and it is a poor service to historical truth to deny their magnitude." [18]

II

If Green had merely advocated a reorientation of Liberal policy on practical grounds, he might still have won an honorable mention in the history of the times. But his real importance lay in the way he linked the new 'positive Liberalism' with a theoretical critique of philosophical doctrines associated with *laissez-faire* Liberalism (and, to a lesser extent, with Toryism) and attempted to re-ground political thinking on the basis of Philosophical Idealism.

The philosophical positions that Green subjected to criticism were various, but most of them had in common a certain orientation that is suggested by the term 'Naturalism.' [19] The two most important theses

[18] Harold J. Laski, *The Decline of Liberalism* (London, 1940), 12.

[19] The target of Green's essay on "Popular Philosophy and Its Relation to Life" (1868) was, collectively, "the doctrines of the Aufklärung [Enlightenment]," which he took to be still the common-denominator "popular philosophy" of the mid-19th

of Naturalism that Green attacked were: (1) the claim that knowledge derived essentially from sense-impressions of the external world, that is, the claim that knowledge was empirical; and (2) the claim that the sole test of the rightness and wrongness of actions was their tendency to promote or diminish happiness, that happiness could be defined as the presence of pleasure and the absence of pain, and that moral conduct could be reduced to something approximating a natural or empirical science.

Against the sensationalist-empiricist theory of knowledge, Green argued that knowledge was possible only because discrete physical sensations were linked in the mind of the perceiving subject by a 'consciousness' or a 'spiritual [i.e., non-natural] principle' that supplied continuity through the succession of sensations and related them according to mental concepts and laws. Sensations provided but the raw material of knowledge, while the human mind supplied the all-important relations among self-impressions and among the 'facts' inferred therefrom. The mind was thus not so much a *tabula rasa* (as Locke had put it), a blank slate upon which the external world wrote

---

century. Singled out for criticism were specific positions held by Hobbes, Locke, Butler, Hume, and Rousseau. In his lengthy "Introductions" to Hume (1874), Green subjected to a systematic critique those principles of Locke's *Essay Concerning Human Understanding* that had received their ultimate logical development in Hume's *Treatise of Human Nature*. In a series of articles published in 1877-78, he shifted his attack to positions held by Herbert Spencer and G. H. Lewes. In the late 1870's he delivered a course of lectures that amounted to a critical examination of J. S. Mill's *Logic*. Finally, in his lectures on the metaphysics of ethics and in the published *Prolegomena to Ethics,* the criticisms were directed at two main targets: evolutionary theorists (such as Spencer) who envisaged a physical 'science of ethics,' and Utilitarians (Bentham, J. S. Mill, Henry Sidgwick) who defended a hedonistic theory of ethics in one form or another.

through the medium of sense-experience, as it was an active participant in the creation of knowledge according to *a priori* concepts and laws. In Green's considered view, there was a good deal of truth in Kant's dictum that 'the understanding makes nature.'[20]   (It is worth noting, in this connection, that Green's most thorough critique of Naturalism took the form of a commentary on Hume. Hume was not only the most penetrating philosopher in the Naturalistic tradition, and therefore the worthiest opponent Green could have chosen; he was also the philosopher who had taken empiricism to its logical extremity and had ended in sceptical conclusions about the very possibility of knowledge, providing thereby the opening for the wedge of epistemological Idealism that Kant and, following him, Green inserted.)

Against the Naturalistic position in ethics, Green made essentially three arguments. One was an *a priori* argument to the effect that moral experience, moral concepts, and moral statements could not logically be reduced to natural or non-moral experience, concepts, or statements, without committing what G. E. Moore was later to call 'the naturalistic fallacy.' In this light, J. S. Mill's celebrated dictum that "the sole evidence it is possible to produce that anything is desirable is that people actually desire it" appears to be, if more than a tautology (and Mill presumably did not intend a tautology), either a pun on the word 'desirable' so that 'capable of being desired' is made to equal 'worthy of being desired,' or else a logical fallacy. As Green pointed out, the fact that a thing is or is not desired is logically irrelevant to whether or not it ought to be desired.[21]

[20] *Prolegomena to Ethics*, Book I, Ch. I.
[21] J. S. Mill, *Utilitarianism*, Ch. IV. Green, *Prolegomena*, §168.

Green's second argument was aimed specifically at the egoistic hedonism of the Utilitarians—at the psychological doctrine that pleasure was the sole or chief thing desired, and at the moral doctrine that pleasure was the sole or chief good worth pursuing, so that men fulfilled their moral duties by pursuing their own pleasure, with the gap between personal pleasure and 'the greatest happiness of the greatest number' being bridged by enlightened self-interest and the pleasures of benevolence. In Green's view, this account simply did not do justice to human experience. It was true that men did seek to some extent to maximize pleasure and minimize pain, and that their social behavior was explicable to some extent in terms of enlightened selfishness and a morality of 'respectability' based on a coincidence of interests. Yet it was simply false psychology to say that pleasure was the sole object of desire; and it did not square with experience to ignore or interpret away the fact that the moral life required the performance of duties and the willing of things as good, regardless of their pleasurableness to the moral agent, and even at times in spite of their painfulness. Hedonism, Green maintained, failed to account satisfactorily for men's consciousness of moral duty and political obligation, for the striving for excellence or virtue, for the conceptions of a 'higher' and a 'lower' self within us and of a 'common good' transcending us, and for the higher reaches of experience in self-sacrificing heroism, patriotism, sainthood, religious exaltation, the creation and appreciation of beauty, and the quest for "the forever (to us) unfilled ideal of a perfect society." [22] There was even some doubt whether it explained the 'ordinary morality' of quiet, everyday dutifulness that

[22] *Works*, I, 369-71; *Prolegomena*, passim.

cemented men's living together in family, church, local community, and state.

If we acknowledge—as Green did not quite do— that Naturalism and Idealism are two diametrically opposite but complementary perspectives, each of which explains the part of human experience near it more directly and satisfactorily, and explains the rest only with some ingenuity, then the issue becomes one of whether the philosopher should take his stand on the lowlands or on the mountains of experience, and from that perspective interpret the rest. On this issue, Green was not in doubt. "Wesley, Wordsworth, Fichte, Mazzini, and the German theologians, lie between us and the generation in which . . . Hume's [philosophy] . . . could be possible," he wrote. "Enthusiasm—religious, political, and poetic—if it has not attained higher forms, has been forced to understand itself better. . . ." [23] From this remark, one might be tempted to conclude that the type of moral experience that the philosopher strove to understand varied from one generation to another. No doubt this is true to some extent, the precise extent being an interesting topic for inquiry. But the main implication of Green's remark points in another direction. It may be instructive at this point for us to recall the case of James Mill, whose anomalous combination of personal asceticism and devotion to the public good with a creed of egoistic hedonism was remarked even by his son. Green counted it to the credit of "the most illustrious spokesmen of Utilitarianism" that "their reforming zeal was too strong" to allow them to act according to their theory of morality.[24]

[23] *Works*, I, 369; III, 117-125.
[24] J. S. Mill, *Autobiography*, Ch. II. Green, *Prolegomena*, §351; *Works*, III, 124.

This brings us to Green's third argument. Although Utilitarianism had done great service in the cause of social and political improvement in the first half of the 19th century, its basic principles had not logically entailed the kind of practical consequences that had been drawn from it. The principle of egoistic hedonism, "if logically carried out," led to social results that the Utilitarian reformers themselves would have disapproved.[25] As time passed, the gap between principle and application became more and more evident, and the usefulness of Utilitarianism as a creed for reformers diminished. In retrospect, we can see that, on the whole, Utilitarianism had served middle-class reformers as a critical weapon for undercutting conservative arguments from historical 'prescription' and for rallying lower-class support for Parliamentary Reform, the repeal of the Corn Laws, and other measures of general beneficence. Once the middle-class reformation of state and society was essentially completed, however, and once the conflict with working-class interests had begun to replace the conflict with aristocratic interests, then the connection between the basic premise of egoistic hedonism and the public formula of 'the greatest happiness of the greatest number' became increasingly tenuous. When the tradition of Radical reform ceased to be inspired by a sense of middle-class self-interest, it could be sustained only by the inspiration of a moral ideal that called for self-sacrifice on behalf of a common good. And when potential supporters of reform were deterred from the path of political Radicalism by repugnance (whether religious, moral, or esthetic) for 'Philosophical Radicalism' (as Utilitarianism was sometimes called), then it was in the interest of political Radicalism to break

[25] *Prolegomena*, Book IV, Chs. III-IV.

with the Utilitarian ethic and ally itself with a more idealistic theory.

That Green's rejection of Utilitarianism and his affirmation of Idealism were tied up with his practical commitment to the on-going tradition of reform can hardly be doubted. Yet this point should not be stressed to the extent of neglecting Green's intense theoretical concern. The inadequacies and incoherences of Utilitarianism, and of Naturalism in general, had become glaring and offensive to the sentiment of rationality, especially as that sentiment was felt by men who required a comprehensive and systematic theory for understanding the world, and not just an action-program for changing it. John Stuart Mill, whose *Autobiography* records in striking form this particular intellectual crisis of 19th-century Britain —the breakdown of the life of practical activity and practical thinking, and the rebirth of the theoretical impulse—had attempted to piece out the narrowness of Benthamism with borrowings from 'the Germano-Coleridgian school' and had virtually compromised away the distinctive characteristics of the Utilitarian viewpoint while still nominally defending it.[26] Mill's urbane eclecticism provided a bridge for minds in transition between two world-views, but it could not satisfy the spiritual hunger that drove a more 'earnest' generation. Since Mill himself had in effect broken with the dogma of *laissez-faire*, the step from Mill to Green was, in *practical* terms, not so large; but, in

---

[26] See: J. S. Mill, *Autobiography*, Ch. V; the essays on "Bertham" and "Coleridge"; *Utilitarianism*, Ch. II, where pleasures are qualitatively distinguished; *On Liberty*, where the argument implicitly passes into the framework of an ethics of self-realization; and *Considerations on Representative Government*, Ch. III, where representative government is judged superior to benevolent despotism on the ground that it fosters a superior character-type.

terms of *theoretical* perspectives, it carried British thought from one world into another.

As an undercurrent in British thought, Idealism can be traced back at least to the 17th-century Cambridge Platonists. But Green's direct roots lay in what Mill had aptly called 'the Germano-Coleridgian school'—the 19th-century British adaptation of perspectives drawn from the philosophy and literature of the age of Kant, Goethe, and Hegel. A complete survey of Green's intellectual debts would also include Aristotle, Protestant mysticism, and the critical, historical approach to theology represented by men like F. C. Baur. Green was not one of those extraordinarily rare, powerfully original thinkers (like Plato or Kant) who initiated genuine philosophical revolutions; but neither was he a mere popularizer. Too independent to be a disciple, but lacking either the vanity or the genius of ultimate originality, he devoted himself to reformulating in his own distinctive way and applying within the context of a modern, industrial, Liberal society, certain principles of classical philosophy and of German Idealism that he judged to be valid, at least more valid than the principles of the current 'popular philosophy.'

In Green's view, the history of philosophy was to be regarded as "a progressive effort towards a fully-articulated conception of the world as rational." The philosopher's task was to make experience intelligible by exhibiting it as a coherent universe whose parts manifested in their different ways the same basic principles. The conception of a rational universe was thus a presupposition inherent in the very conception of philosophy. The aim of philosophy was not so much to go beyond experience as to explain experience; but, since not all experience was sense-experience, not all philosophical statements about the struc-

ture of experience were "sensibly verifiable," and
even less "sensibly verifiable" were the logical explora-
tions of the conditions presupposed by the possibility
of experience.[27]

The intellectual dilemma of the age, as Green saw
it, lay in the fact that the traditional Christian overview had become discredited in its dogmatic form,
partly due to the rise of scientific thinking, while
scientific theories were barred by their very nature
(i.e., their dependence upon empirical or sensible
verification) from providing a comprehensive, integral
theory of experience. The result was a bifurcated
culture: men gave allegiance to scientific ideas on the
one hand, while on the other they continued to live
in a seemingly incompatible world of moral, religious,
and esthetic experience that was articulated in poetry
and religion. The resulting 'speculative misery' felt
even by 'practical men' could be solaced only by a
philosophical overview that created wholeness through
systematizing these scattered insights and delineating
the spheres within which the different realms of dis-
course (e.g., poetry and science) were applicable.[28]
Such a philosophical synthesis was possible, Green
correctly saw, only on the basis of Idealist principles.
The intellectual dilemma that made Idealism welcome
in Britain thus reduplicated in its essentials the dilemma of German intellectual life in the age of Hegel.
We are in the presence here of the modern form of a
perennial, archetypal conception of philosophy, which
arises out of man's recurring need to overcome the
separations and contradictions of empirical existence
and ordinary thought. Through theoretical activity
the philosopher strives (in the phrases Green used)

[27] *Works*, I, 1-5, 449; *Prolegomena*, §2 and passim.
[28] *Prolegomena*, §1.

to discover himself "ever at home" in the world, and to win "the freedom of perfect understanding."

For a full acquaintance with the way Green worked out the philosophical task he set himself, one must read the *Prolegomena to Ethics*. The most that can be attempted here is a brief sketch of the several layers of meaning implied by the term 'Idealism' as it applies to Green, in the hope that this will make it easier to understand *The Principles of Political Obligation*.

First of all, Green's Idealism involved a theory of knowledge stressing the active, formative role of the human mind in structuring its experience. But when Green reflected on the problems left by Kant, he found himself led on to adopt the basic principle of Hegelian metaphysics, the postulate of an ultimate 'spiritual principle' underlying, and manifesting itself in, the patterns of our mental activity, the structure of nature, and the political-social-cultural configurations of man's historical existence.[29] This postulate made it possible to interpret life teleologically in terms of a two-fold process of 'realization,' whereby the spiritual principle, existing as potency, achieved through the practical activity of men an objective embodiment in the world of institutions, and achieved through the intellectual activity of men a consciousness of itself as the fundamental principle structuring the universe.

This second or contemplative aspect of the process of realization was represented in the Idealistic *esthetic* that Green opposed to Naturalistic theories of art. It was the achievement of great art not so much to describe the externally observable characteristics of things as to penetrate their inner reality, their indwell-

[29] *Works,* III, 141-146.

ing potential rationality, and to portray this in sensuous or verbal form for contemplation. The parallel to this in Green's political theory was a focus on the inner "idea of the state," on "what it is in tendency or idea," which did not preclude (indeed, it made possible) an awareness of the gap between ideal essence and empirical existence, the extent to which an institution like the state could be "inconsistent with its idea." [30]

The other aspect of the process of realization was represented in Green's *moral* Idealism—his conception of the essentially moral nature and vocation of man and of the institutions that man created, inhabited, and continually re-formed. With all due respect to the 'natural' factors conditioning moral and political life, the central realities of these spheres of experience were 'ideal realities,' intangible shared ideas (like the good, rights, the state) that had their existence ultimately in the minds of men. What distinguished man from the rest of creation was the capacity for using reason to set goals for satisfying the enduring moral self, and to will these goals even at the sacrifice of pleasurable sensations. Deviating from the Kantian ethics of 'duty for duty's sake,' Green stressed the purposive or teleological character of moral activity: the important thing was whether an action contributed (both in intention and in effect) to the greater realization of human capacities in ourselves and in others. The moral basis of the claim to rights in society lay in the capacity for self-development implicit in every individual. But because moral progress was something inward, a condition of the will, as well as something expressing itself in outward forms, it was not something that could be produced by force

[30] *Works,* III, 20ff. *Principles of Political Obligation,* §§121ff., §§132ff., §§142f., §148, §221.

impinging from without. And force was unavoidably
implied in state action. Hence, although political
obligation was grounded in a conception of the moral
good, the state could not legitimately act directly to
enforce virtue, but played its role indirectly by removing obstacles to the free development of human faculties. Such, in brief, was the foundation of Philosophical Idealism in which Green's political theory was
rooted.

It was due to Green more than to any other single
person that the Idealist standpoint came to dominate
British philosophy, spreading from Oxford in the
1870's and 1880's to the Scottish Universities and to
the literature and educated consciousness of the age.
Different philosophical tendencies, critical of Idealism
and hostile to its spirit of speculative synthesis, began
to appear in the opening years of the 20th century;
but the reign of Idealism was definitively overthrown
only by the rising tide of anti-German feeling that
reached its peak during World War I. Since then,
in a period dominated by Philosophical Analysis, Logical Positivism, and Linguistic Philosophy, the prestige
of Idealism has been at low tide. Green's metaphysics
and epistemology were the first parts of his philosophy
to fall into discredit; his ethics lingered longer; and
the type of political philosophy that he initiated has
remained alive, though scarcely dominant, to the
present day.[31] By the 1960's there were signs that the
reaction against Idealism had about run its course.
Voices had begun to be heard protesting that the
function of philosophy was not merely analysis but
also synthesis and perhaps also practical guidance;
that science was one thing and philosophy another;
and that an exclusive preoccupation with language
restricted philosophy to a rather superficial level.

[31] See Section V of the Bibliography.

And interest—a sympathetic interest—began to be directed once more to Hegel, Green, and Bradley.

III

It is not hard to discover deficiencies in Green's thought. On the practical level, the weaknesses were typical of the 'positive' phase of Liberal Radicalism as a whole. Bold insights into social problems and bold statements of principle were followed by cautiously modest proposals. For example, Green was himself one of "those who hold that universal ownership is a condition of moral well-being," but he could not bring himself to sanction interference with "freedom of bequest." [32] In actual practice, in order to raise the standard of living in the cities to the level Green thought desirable, it was necessary for the state to provide social services financed in part out of progressive taxation; yet Green seemed to be of two minds about publicly provided social services, and he discussed taxation only in connection with the state's right to encourage cultivation of the land (presumably by levying heavy taxes on unused land) and in connection with a possibly confiscatory tax on 'unearned increment' (which he feared might diminish the proprietors' incentive to 'make the most of the land').[33] And Green—even though he, more than anyone else, turned the attention of British Liberalism to the problems of the industrial wage-earner—still exhibited something of the anachronism that crippled Liberal Radicalism as a political force: the tendency to talk as if the problems of the industrial working class could

[32] *Principles of Political Obligation*, §§224ff.
[33] *Ibid.*, §§17f., §224, §232.

be dealt with by blaming, or passing legislation against, the rural landowners.

Finally, Green had something of the typical Liberal Radical's over-optimistic faith in 'the people'—as if the average man were straining at the leash with zeal for moral self-improvement, self-culture, and the responsibilities of active citizenship. Reformers ignore at their peril the insight of Tory Democracy: most people want to enjoy their private lives and leave politics to others to carry on in their behalf. Green was not as naive as some ardent democrats: he was aware that the right of political participation tended to become less valued the more widely it was shared; he noted tendencies towards what might today be called 'mass culture' and 'mass society;' and he did not support political democratization out of any conviction that 'the people' were always right in their judgment. He did suffer disappointment, however, over the use made by workingmen of the leisure that legislation was beginning to secure them. His strictures on "the general riot of luxury" enjoyed by the populace during a short-lived commercial boom remind one of the reaction of some Socialists to the advent of the 'affluent society' of the 1950's: the same Puritan strain becomes apparent.[34] When Green realized that better material conditions did not of themselves bring an immediate end to the chronic drunkenness that had become an opiate for the miseries of the Industrial Revolution, he turned to the ideas of compulsory temperance legislation; and it was here that he came nearest to violating his own guiding principle that the state could not enforce virtue.

On the theoretical level, Green's criticisms of Utilitarianism have by now become part of the common

[34] *Works,* III, cxviii.

educated consciousness. But his own philosophy was not without difficulties. We may grant Green his conception of the task of philosophy and his Idealist standpoint as legitimate perspectives, while still saying of his philosophy what he said of Hegel's:

On reflection we become aware that we are Hegelians, so to speak, with only a fraction of our thoughts—on the Sundays of 'speculation,' not on the weekdays of 'ordinary thought;' and even if we silence all suspicion as to the truth and value of the 'speculation,' we still feel the need of some . . . mediation between speculative truth and our judgments concerning matters of fact. . . .[35]

The postulation of an absolute 'spiritual principle' to explain the possibility of a self's knowing and acting in a world of nature and of other selves, seems in retrospect only to substitute one mystery for another. The adoption of an ethics of self-realization raises the issue of how the 'self' that should be realized is to be defined, the issue of *which* 'capabilities' and 'faculties' one ought to develop, and of how the discriminations involved in a definition of a 'true self' can be justified. Rhetoric about 'the higher faculties' and 'the best that is in us' no doubt conveys a certain meaning in a particular cultural context, but it is not philosophically enlightening. Again, on the crucial question of the nature of 'the good'—e.g., just what is it that the 'good will' wills?—one detects elements of circularity and even evasiveness in Green's arguments. Finally, although it is understandably not in the nature of an absolute Idealism to acknowledge conflict rather than harmony as ultimate, one could still wish for a greater appreciation of the tragic character of life on the existential level—the inescapable

[35] *Works*, III, 142.

conflicts among 'capabilities' not all of which can be realized, the occasional incompatibilities between different moral duties, the tension between conventional morality and the reflective moral consciousness, and the dilemma of the person torn between the duty of the good man and the obligation of the good citizen. Perhaps in 'the best of all possible worlds' or in 'the heavenly city' such conflicts would not exist, but meanwhile they structure a good deal of our moral and political experience. A philosophy that aspires either to explain or to guide experience must be careful to do them justice.

There remains something unfinished about Green's philosophy. How much this is due to his relatively early death, how much to the intrinsic difficulty of the task he set himself, and how much to the limits of his intellectual powers, could no doubt be debated at length. If the value of a philosophy consists partly in its degree of technical perfection, it consists also partly in the degree to which it satisfies the needs that give rise to the philosophical enterprise. It was the merit of Green's philosophy that it grappled with both the central theoretical dilemma and the central practical dilemma of the time: the tension between the claims of science and historical criticism, on the one hand, and the claims of morality, religion, and poetry, on the other; and the tension between the political and social ideals associated with two antagonistic classes. On the theoretical level, Green was concerned that the capacity for an overall, unifying perspective on experience should not be lost; and on the practical level, he was concerned that the framework of political community should not be shattered. Whatever reservations one may have about Green's precise resolution of the theoretical problem, one cannot but be grateful for his having kept the task of

philosophical synthesis from disappearing from view
in an age when philosophers had already begun to
take refuge in technical exercises, and the role of theoretical unification had already begun to be usurped
by uncritical ideologies and political myths. And,
whatever reservations one may have about Green's
political program, one cannot deny that he faced with
exemplary realism the dilemma of 19th-century Liberalism and exercised his influence in a beneficent direction.

In the last analysis, the secret of Green's appeal lies
as much in the spirit of his life as in the letter of his
teaching. The appreciations written by men who
knew him strike a common note: admiration for the
versatility and the wholeness of his life and work.
Green was not merely a scholar, but a philosopher
who undertook the responsibility of thinking through
for himself the nature of experience. He was not
merely a subject interested in politics, but a citizen
who took on the duties of democratic self-government
and active social reform. And somehow he managed
to weave these two roles of philosopher and citizen
into an integral pattern of life. "Metaphysicians,"
observed James Bryce, who had known Green at Balliol, "are generally as little interested in practical
politics as poets are, and not better suited for practical life. Green was a remarkable exception. Politics were in a certain sense the strongest of his interests. . . . Green will be long remembered . . . as a
singular instance of a metaphysician with a bent towards politics and practical life. . . ." [36] There was a
symbolic story told of Green to the effect that "He
went straight from the declaration of the poll, when
he was elected a town councillor, to lecture on *The*

[36] James Bryce, *Studies in Contemporary Biography* (New
York and London, 1903), 97, 99.

Critique of Pure Reason." [37] And it was remarked by many that when Green died, he was mourned by Oxford the town as well as by Oxford the university. These were the things that became legendary. They amount, after all, to nothing other than a striking embodiment, at one particular time and place, of the vision of a fully developed and integral humanity, which has been perennially represented by the distinctive intellectual activity that we call 'Political Theory.'

Political Theory is inspired by a double passion. On the one hand, it is driven by an impulse to understand and appreciate the nature of things political and their place in the world of experience, to achieve reconciliation through contemplation (*theoria*). On the other hand, it is driven by an impulse to affect and transform the very things contemplated, to achieve reconciliation through practical activity (or at least through the advocacy of it). Even the more contemplative political theorists (such as Aristotle and St. Thomas Aquinas) have betrayed a wish to influence the way political things are to be; and even those most obviously driven by the urge to affect events (such as Machiavelli and Burke) have betrayed a secret, disinterested delight in the sheer understanding of the processes of politics and their place in the world. These contemplative and practical themes— the extent to which Political Theory is *theory* and the extent to which it is *political*—have intertwined in a multitude of ways in the history of Political Theory. The tension between these two fundamental and contrary orientations towards life, together with the struggle to integrate them in a coherent outlook, comprises the unending drama, at once futile and ennobling, that lies at the heart of the enterprise of

[37] D. G. Ritchie, *Principles of State Inference* (London, 1891), 131.

Political Theory and constitutes the interest that it
has for all men.

It has become common in recent years to lament
'the decline of Political Theory' and to blame this
decline on the tendency for intellectuals to withdraw
from active interest in political affairs into mere schol-
arship.[38] With equal plausibility, however, one might
attribute the decline to the widespread assumption by
intellectuals that (in Marx's words) "Philosophers
have only *interpreted* the world in various ways; the
point however is to *change* it." [39]   In short, there
seems to have been a gradual desertion of the theoretical enterprise carried on for its own sake, and an
increasing preoccupation with practice-oriented, instrumental thinking. This trend is observable not
only in the case of Marxism, but also with Utilitarianism, Pragmatism, Existentialism, and virtually every
intellectual movement in the last 150 years.   Which-
ever explanation is truer, the fact that each can be
supported with evidence, as well as the fact that each
explanation presupposes a definition of Political Theory that the other explanation points to as a 'decline' of
Political Theory, suggests that theoretical and practical tendencies have become maladjusted, and that
there is an increasing polarization between theoretical
and practical thinking which threatens the continuation of Political Theory and of the humane vision that
it has represented.

In this context, it may be instructive to recall the
example of T. H. Green. Those who deplore im-
practical academics can honor him as a theorist with
a passion for practical politics and a knowledge of its
problems, as a theorist who regarded as a symptom of

---

[38] See the influential essay by Alfred Cobban, "The Decline
of Political Theory" (*Political Science Quarterly*, 1953).
[39] "Theses on Feuerbach," XI.

political decadence Aristotle's ideal of the good life as
pure contemplation.[40] Those who deplore the tri-
umph of pragmatic man can praise Green for attempting a radical re-theorization of political thinking, for
reviving the theoretical enterprise as something legitimate in its own right, and for reminding us that "man,
above all the modern man, must theorize his practice,
and the failure adequately to do so, must cripple the
practice itself." [41] Green was well aware that "the
old antagonism between speculation and action" had
taken on in modern industrial society a greater in-
tensity, that in an age of "the progressive division of
labour, . . . we seem to lose our completeness as
men." [42] The unity of his own life, which belied this
fate, has thus the significance of something not merely
given, accidental, or fortunate, but artfully won. His
epitaph might come from his philosophy:

The common element to both [theoretical speculation
and practical willing] lies in the consciousness of a self
and a world as in a sense opposed to each other, and in
the conscious effort to overcome this opposition. . . .
One [i.e., speculation] is the effort of such consciousness
to take the world into itself, the other [i.e., willing] its
effort to carry itself out into the world. . . . Neither
action can really be exerted without calling the other into
play.[43]

The coherence that Green established between the
contemplative and practical dimensions of his Political
Theory was not, of course, purely a logical coherence.
Between metaphysical postulates and political advice
there is not only the mediation of other propositions,

---

[40] *Works*, III, 89f.
[41] *Works*, III, 124.
[42] *Works*, III, 35, 40.
[43] *Prolegomena*, §130, §136, §135.

but also frequently a logical gulf. Every political theorist is apt to overestimate the extent to which his recommendations follow from his first principles, and Green was no exception. The coherence of a Political Theory is more a matter of an absence of inconsistencies, an artistic achievement, a unity of mood and perspective. One interpretation locates the vital key to Green's life and thought in his religious background;[44] yet to stress this is to focus on what Green had in common with his contemporaries, rather than to single out what distinguished him. The absolute 'spiritual principle,' which Green sometimes evoked in quasi-religious terminology, had its precursors not only in religious conceptions of the deity but also in the speculations of philosophers ancient and modern. Green's 'religion' was essentially that of a philosopher and a moralist: by defining 'God' as man's idea of a fully realized moral being, he presumed the priority of morals to religion, and of moral philosophy to theology. The anguish of the truly religious thinkers of the last 100 years (Dostoevsky, Nietzsche, Sartre) —'If God is dead, then everything is permitted'—was totally outside Green's frame of reference. Beneath the variations of time and place and personality— Green's Englishness, his Victorian attitudes, his nominal membership in the Church of England, and all the rest—there flowed once again the age-old tradition of the moral philosopher concerned to reflect on man's moral experience as manifested in institutional and in personal life, to make the principles thereof explicit, and to criticize or raise the standard of the Ideal when needed.

In the tradition of Political Theory, it was moral philosophy that ruled the theoretical realm and pro-

---

[44] See Melvin Richter, *The Politics of Conscience: T. H. Green and His Times* (London, 1964).

vided the bridge to the practical side. A period of 'decline' for Political Theory is invariably a period when other things usurp the sovereign place of moral philosophy: theology in the Middle Ages; science, history, psychology, and merely practical thinking today. Interpretations of what was, what recurs, or what cause has what effects, however, yield no purposive justification or imperative unless some moral philosophy has been tacitly presupposed. Utilitarianism, Marxism, Fabianism, and Evolutionary theories of politics all tried to evade or play down, in one way or another, the inescapable moral issue. T. H. Green succeeded for a brief moment in bringing political thinking back to the central issue of moral justification. In the course of the horrors of the 20th century, moral questions have come to the fore again in a way that no honest man can ignore. In this context, too, it may be helpful to recall T. H. Green, who faced openly the need for Political Theory to be grounded in moral philosophy. We will not find in Green any ready or final answers to our questions, but we may be led to re-acquaint ourselves with that activity of reflecting on practical activity called 'moral philosophy,' the reawakening of which is a precondition for the true revival of Political Theory in our time.

A NOTE ON THE SELECTIONS

The text of the historic lecture on *Liberal Legislation and Freedom of Contract,* which Green himself published as a pamphlet, is reprinted in full. I have not hesitated, however, to cut the lectures on "The Senses of 'Freedom'" and *The Principles of Political Obligation,* which Green did not revise for publication. The full text of *The Principles of Political Obli-*

gation is particularly repetitive, partly because of Green's method of exhibiting the same basic principles in a variety of contexts, but also simply because of the normal character of lectures not edited by their author for publication. In making the selections, I have tried to include everything essential for an understanding of the basic principles of Green's Idealist political theory, and to show these principles in application to Green's central practical concern, 'the social question.'

The arrangement of the three selections is not strictly chronological. This raises no problem, however, since all three come from the years 1879-81 and comprise, in effect, Green's last reflections on politics, and since Green's thinking developed without undergoing any great conversions or changes of direction. Nor is the arrangement dictated by logic, for a political theory forms a circle that one may enter either at the practical or at the theoretical side. *Liberal Legislation and Freedom of Contract* is placed first simply because we are apt to enter more easily into a political theory through the door of practical thinking. In this context, the theoretical issue of the nature of freedom arises naturally. The second selection, "The Senses of 'Freedom,'" continues the consideration of this issue, although in a different key: the effort to persuade gives way to a quest for theoretical clarification. Finally, with *The Principles of Political Obligation,* we enter upon a comprehensive examination, from the standpoint of moral philosophy, of the principles implicit in the political life of the modern liberal-democratic state. The concern with freedom, overt in the first two selections, should not be missed in the third. A little reflection on the text of *The Principles of Political Obligation* will suggest that these lectures might just as appropriately have been titled "The Principles of Political Freedom." Their central preoccupation is with rights, which are the concrete forms that freedom takes in political society; and Green is quite explicit that "the objects for which government subsists" are "the general *freedom* of action and acquisition and self-development," and that "political society is more complete as the *freedom* guaranteed is more complete, both in respect of the persons enjoying it and of the range of possible action and acquisition over which it extends." [45]

These selections provide Green's controversial notion of 'positive freedom' with both its strategic and its philosophic context. On analysis, the notion of 'positive freedom' (as it is defined in *Liberal Legislation and Freedom of Contract*) will be found to combine several distinguishable elements, not all of which are essential to Green's political purpose. Various of these elements are discussed in the other two selections, but the reader should beware of assuming a complete identity. Among other things, it is necessary to distinguish what is permissible in a political speech from what is permissible in an academic lecture in philosophy, and Green will be found to have kept these levels tolerably distinct, as a comparison of the first two selections on the use of the term 'freedom' will show. Finally, it may be useful in appraising Green's discussion of freedom, to keep in mind the distinction between linguistic, logical, and phenomenological levels of analysis. Before dismissing the notion of 'positive freedom' as a linguistic confusion or a 'persuasive definition' (a definition craftily retaining the favorable emotive connotation of the

---

[45] *Principles of Political Obligation,* §108, §91. Editor's emphasis.

word 'freedom' while shifting its descriptive meaning); and before dismissing it on the ground that it is the answer to a question that is logically distinct from the question to which the notion of 'negative freedom' is the answer; it is necessary to consider whether there is any essential connection in the structure of experience between the absence of constraint ('negative freedom') and any of the elements (or the total syndrome) of what Green meant by 'positive freedom.' One such connection is suggested in §18 of "The Senses of 'Freedom,'" where Green observes that "the feeling of oppression, which always goes along with the consciousness of unfulfilled possibilities, will always give meaning to the representation of the effort after any kind of self-improvement as a demand for 'freedom.'" It is on this level, though not necessarily with this particular point, that the re-thinking of the controversy over 'positive freedom' ought to begin.

Footnotes to the selections are the editor's, except when specified otherwise. Green's spelling (e.g., 'proletariate') and punctuation have generally been retained, except for a few clear lapses, which have been corrected.

J.R.R.

PRINCIPAL DATES IN THE LIFE
OF THOMAS HILL GREEN

1836 Born, the son of the Rev. Valentine Green, rector of Birkin, Yorkshire, England.

1850-55 Educated at Rugby.

1855-59 Educated at Balliol College, Oxford, where his tutor was Benjamin Jowett.

1860-82 Taught at Oxford. Beginning as a Lecturer in ancient and modern history at Balliol, Green soon passed to lecturing on the New Testament and, increasingly, on philosophical texts, especially Aristotle's *Ethics*. A Fellow of Balliol from 1861, and Tutor of Balliol from 1866, he was elected Whyte's Professor of Moral Philosophy in the University of Oxford in 1878. In this last capacity he delivered the courses of lectures published posthumously as *Prolegomena to Ethics* and *The Principles of Political Obligation*.

1862-63 Summer vacations spent in Germany.

1865-66 Assistant Commissioner, Schools Inquiry Commission.

1871 Married Charlotte Symonds. Became an Oxford householder and therefore eligible to participate in town politics.

1874 "Introductions" to Hume's *Treatise of Human Nature* published. Elected to town School Board.

1876 Elected to Town Council, representing the North Ward.

1881 Lecture on "Liberal Legislation and Freedom of Contract" delivered at Leicester.

1882 Died, following an illness, in his 47th year, leaving the *Prolegomena to Ethics* almost completed for publication.

LIBERAL LEGISLATION
AND FREEDOM OF CONTRACT[1]

THAT a discussion on this subject is opportune will hardly be disputed by any one who noticed the line of argument by which at least two of the liberal measures of last session[2] were opposed. To the Ground Game Act it was objected that it interfered with freedom of contract between landlord and tenant. It withdrew the sanction of law from any agreement by which the occupier of land should transfer to the owner the exclusive right of killing hares and rabbits on the land in his occupation. The Employers' Liability Act was objected to on similar grounds. It did not indeed go the length of preventing masters and workmen from contracting themselves out of its operation. But it was urged that it went on the wrong principle of encouraging the workman to look to the law for the protection which he ought to secure for himself by voluntary contract. 'The workman,' it was argued, 'should be left to take care of himself by the

[1] A lecture delivered to the Liberal Association of Leicester, England, early in 1881; printed as a pamphlet the same year. The text here is reprinted in full from Green's *Works*, Vol. III, pages 365-386. The immediate context was the controversy over the land question in Ireland (see note 16 below). Ireland was at this time, of course, part of the United Kingdom of Great Britain and Ireland, was represented in Parliament at Westminster, and was subject to the enactments of Parliament. On the meaning of the terms 'liberal legislation' and 'freedom of contract,' see the Note at the end of this selection.

[2] The *last session* of Parliament, Summer 1880.

terms of his agreement with the employer. It is not
for the state to step in and say, as by the new act it
says, that when a workman is hurt in carrying out
the instructions of the employer or his foreman, the
employer, in the absence of a special agreement to the
contrary, shall be liable for compensation. If the
law thus takes to protecting men, whether tenant-
farmers, or pitmen,[3] or railway servants, who ought
to be able to protect themselves, it tends to weaken
their self-reliance, and thus, in unwisely seeking to do
them good, it lowers them in the scale of moral beings.'

Such is the language which was everywhere in the
air last summer, and which many of us, without being
convinced by it, may have found it difficult to answer.
The same line of objection is equally applicable to
other legislation of recent years, to our factory acts,
education acts, and laws relating to public health.
They all, in one direction or another, limit a man's
power of doing what he will with what he considers
his own. They all involve the legal prohibition of
certain agreements between man and man, and as
there is nothing to force men into these agreements,
it might be argued that, supposing them to be mischievous, men would, in their own interest, gradually
learn to refuse them. There is other legislation which
the liberal party is likely to demand, and which is
sure to be objected to on the same ground, with what
justice we shall see as we proceed. If it is proposed
to give the Irish tenant some security in his holding,
to save him from rack-renting[4] and from the confiscation of the results of his labour in the improvement
of the soil, it will be objected that in so doing the
state goes out of its way to interfere with the contracts, possibly beneficial to both sides, which land-

---

[3] *Pitmen:* mineworkers.
[4] *Rack-renting:* imposing exorbitantly high rents.

lord and tenant would otherwise make with each other. Leave the tenant, it will be said, to secure himself by contract. Meanwhile the demand for greater security of tenure is growing stronger amongst our English farmers, and should it be proposed—as it must before this parliament expires—to give legal effect to it, the proposal will be met by the same cry, that it is an interference with the freedom of contract, unless, indeed, like Lord Beaconsfield's Act of 1875,[5] it undoes with one hand what it professes to do with the other.

There are two other matters with which the liberal leaders have virtually promised to deal, and upon which they are sure to be met by an appeal to the supposed inherent right of every man to do what he will with his own. One is the present system of settling land, the other the liquor traffic. The only effectual reform of the land laws is to put a stop to those settlements or bequests by which at present a landlord may prevent a successor from either converting any part of his land into money or from dividing it among his children. But if it is proposed to take away from the landlord this power of hampering posterity, it will be said to be an interference with his free disposal of his property. As for the liquor traffic, it is obvious that even the present licensing laws, ineffectual as some of us think them, interfere with the free sale of an article in large consumption, and that with the concession of 'local option' the interference would, to say the least, be probably carried much further. I have said enough to show that the most pressing political questions of our time are questions of which the settlement, I do not say necessarily involves an interference with freedom of contract, but

[5] *Lord Beaconsfield's* [Disraeli's] *Act of 1875:* presumably, the Artisans' Dwelling Act.

is sure to be resisted in the sacred name of individual
liberty, not only by all those who are interested in
keeping things as they are, but by others to whom
freedom is dear for its own sake, and who do not
sufficiently consider the conditions of its maintenance
in such a society as ours. In this respect there is a
noticeable difference between the present position of
political reformers and that in which they stood a generation ago. Then they fought the fight of reform in
the name of individual freedom against class privilege. Their opponents could not with any plausibility invoke the same name against them. Now, in
appearance—though, as I shall try to show, not in
reality—the case is changed. The nature of the genuine political reformer is perhaps always the same.
The passion for improving mankind, in its ultimate
object, does not vary. But the immediate object of
reformers, and the forms of persuasion by which they
seek to advance them, vary much in different generations. To a hasty observer they might even seem
contradictory, and to justify the notion that nothing
better than a desire for change, selfish or perverse, is
at the bottom of all reforming movements. Only
those who will think a little longer about it can discern the same old cause of social good against class
interests, for which, under altered names, liberals are
fighting now as they were fifty years ago.

Our political history since the first reform act naturally falls into three divisions. [1] The first, beginning with the reform of parliament, and extending to
Sir R. Peel's administration[6] is marked by the struggle
of free society against close privileged corporations.

[6] That is, from the Reform Act of 1832, which shifted Parliamentary representation somewhat from the countryside to the
towns and slightly extended the franchise, up to the beginning
of the 1841-46 Government of the Conservative Prime Minister,
Sir Robert Peel (1788-1850).

Its greatest achievement was the establishment of representative municipal governments in place of the close bodies which had previously administered the affairs of our cities and boroughs; a work which after an interval of nearly half a century we hope shortly to see extended to the rural districts. Another important work was the overhauling the immense charities of the country, and the placing them under something like adequate public control. And the natural complement of this was the removal of the grosser abuses in the administration of the church, the abolition of pluralities and sinecures, and the reform of cathedral chapters. In all this, while there was much that contributed to the freedom of our civil life, there was nothing that could possibly be construed as an interference with the rights of the individual. No one was disturbed in doing what he would with his own. Even those who had fattened on abuses had their vested interests duly respected, for the house of commons then as now had 'quite a passion for compensation.' [2] With the ministry of Sir R. Peel began the struggle of society against monopolies; in other words, the liberation of trade. Some years later Mr. Gladstone, in his famous budgets, was able to complete the work which his master began, and it is now some twenty years since the last vestige of protection for any class of traders or producers disappeared. The taxes on knowledge, as they were called, followed the taxes on food, and since most of us grew up there has been no exchangeable commodity in England except land—no doubt a large exception—of which the exchange has not been perfectly free.[7]

---

[7] Under Peel's Prime Ministership, the Corn Laws (tariffs on grain) were repealed, and tariffs on many other imports (particularly foodstuffs) were drastically reduced. William

The realisation of complete freedom of contract was the special object of this reforming work. It was to set men at liberty to dispose of what they had made their own that the free-trader worked. He only interfered to prevent interference. He would put restraint on no man in doing anything that did not directly check the free dealing of some one in something else. [3] But of late reforming legislation has taken, as I have pointed out, a seemingly different direction. It has not at any rate been so readily identifiable with the work of liberation. In certain respects it has put restraints on the individual in doing what he will with his own. And it is noticeable that this altered tendency begins, in the main, with the more democratic parliament of 1868.[8] It is true that the earlier factory acts, limiting as they do by law the conditions under which certain kinds of labour may be bought and sold, had been passed some time before. The first approach to an effectual factory act dates as far back as the time of the first reform act, but it only applied to the cotton industry, and was very imperfectly put in force.[9] It aimed at limiting the hours of labour for children and young persons. Gradually the limitation of hours came to be enforced, other industries were brought under the operation of the restraining laws, and the same protection extended

Ewart *Gladstone* (1809-1898) had been Peel's chief lieutenant in these 'free trade' reforms, then had gravitated into the Liberal Party after the Conservatives split over the Corn Law issue. As Chancellor of the Exchequer subsequently, he continued Peel's work; he later served four times as Prime Minister and held this office at the time of Green's lecture.

[8] The *Parliament of 1868* had been elected on the basis of the more democratic franchise resulting from the Reform Act of 1867 carried by Disraeli.

[9] This was the *Factory Act* of 1833, which succeeded the relatively ineffective Acts of 1802 and 1816.

to women as to young persons. But it was only alongside of the second reform act in 1867 that an attempt was made by parliament to apply the same rule to every kind of factory and workshop; only later still, in the first parliament elected partly by household suffrage, that efficient measures were taken for enforcing the restraints which previous legislation had in principle required. Improvements and extensions in detail have since been introduced, largely through the influence of Mr. Mundella,[10] and now we have a system of law by which, in all our chief industries except the agricultural, the employment of children except as half-timers is effectually prevented, the employment of women and young persons is effectually restricted to ten hours a day, and in all places of employment health and bodily safety have all the protection which rules can give them.

If factory regulation had been attempted, though only in a piecemeal way, some time before we had a democratic house of commons, the same cannot be said of educational law. It was the parliament elected by a more popular suffrage in 1868 that passed, as we know, the first great education act. That act introduced compulsory schooling. It left the compulsion, indeed, optional with local school-boards, but compulsion is the same in principle, is just as much compulsion by the state, whether exercised by the central government or delegated by that government to provincial authorities. The education act of 1870 was a wholly new departure in English legislation, though Mr. Forster was wise enough to proceed ten-

[10] Anthony John *Mundella* (1825-97): Liberal Radical politician active in behalf of factory legislation and public education. He entered Gladstone's second Government in 1880 as Vice-President of the Council in charge of education.

tatively, and leave the adoption of compulsory bye-laws to the discretion of school-boards.[11] It was so just as much as if he had attempted at once to enforce compulsory attendance through the action of the central government. The principle was established once for all that parents were not to be allowed to do as they willed with their children, if they willed either to set them to work or to let them run wild without elementary education. Freedom of contract in respect of all dealings with the labour of children was so far limited.

I need not trouble you with recalling the steps by which the principle of the act of 1870 has since been further applied and enforced. It is evident that in the body of school and factory legislation which I have noticed we have a great system of interference with freedom of contract. The hirer of labour is prevented from hiring it on terms to which the person of whom he hires it could for the most part have been readily brought to agree. If children and young persons and women were not ready in many cases, either from their own wish, or under the influence of parents and husbands, to accept employment of the kind which the law prohibits, there would have been no occasion for the prohibition. It is true that adult men are not placed directly under the same restriction. The law does not forbid them from working as long hours as they please. But I need not point out here that in effect the prevention of the employment of juvenile labour beyond certain hours, amounts, at least in the textile industries, to the prevention of the working of machinery beyond those hours. It thus indirectly puts a limit on the number of hours during

---

[11] *The Education Act of 1870*, dealing with elementary education, was largely the work of W. E. *Forster* (1818-86), then Vice-President of the Council in Gladstone's first Government.

which the manufacturer can employ his men. And if it is only accidentally, so to speak, that the hiring of men's labour is interfered with by the half-time and ten hours' system, the interference on grounds of health and safety is as direct as possible. The most mature man is prohibited by law from contracting to labour in factories, or pits, or workshops, unless certain rules for the protection of health and limb are complied with. In like manner he is prohibited from living in a house which the sanitary inspector pronounces unwholesome. The free sale or letting of a certain kind of commodity is thereby prevented. Here, then, is a great system of restriction, which yet hardly any impartial person wishes to see reversed; which many of us wish to see made more complete. Perhaps, however, we have never thoroughly considered the principles on which we approve it. It may be well, therefore, to spend a short time in ascertaining those principles. We shall then be on surer ground in approaching those more difficult questions of legislation which must shortly be dealt with, and of which the settlement is sure to be resisted in the name of individual liberty.

We shall probably all agree that freedom, rightly understood, is the greatest of blessings; that its attainment is the true end of all our effort as citizens. But when we thus speak of freedom, we should consider carefully what we mean by it. We do not mean merely freedom from restraint or compulsion. We do not mean merely freedom to do as we like irrespectively of what it is that we like. We do not mean a freedom that can be enjoyed by one man or one set of men at the cost of a loss of freedom to others. When we speak of freedom as something to be so highly prized, we mean a positive power or capacity of doing or enjoying something worth doing or enjoying, and that, too, something that we do or enjoy in common with others. We mean by it a power which each man exercises through the help or security given him by his fellow-men, and which he in turn helps to secure for them. When we measure the progress of a society by its growth in freedom, we measure it by the increasing development and exercise on the whole of those powers of contributing to social good with which we believe the members of the society to be endowed; in short, by the greater power on the part of the citizens as a body to make the most and best of themselves. Thus, though of course there can be no freedom among men who act not willingly but under compulsion, yet on the other hand the mere removal of compulsion, the mere enabling a man to do as he likes, is in itself no contribution to true freedom. In one sense no man is so well able to do as he likes as the wandering savage. He has no master. There is no one to say him nay. Yet we do not count him really free, because the freedom of savagery is not strength, but weakness. The actual powers of the noblest savage do not admit of comparison with those of the humblest citizen of a law-abiding state. He is not the slave of man, but he is the slave of nature. Of compulsion by natural necessity he has plenty of experience, though of restraint by society none at all. Nor can he deliver himself from that compulsion except by submitting to this restraint. So to submit is the first step in true freedom, because the first step towards the full exercise of the faculties with which man is endowed. But we rightly refuse to recognise the highest development on the part of an exceptional individual or exceptional class, as an advance towards the true freedom of man, if it is founded on a refusal of the same opportunity to other men. The powers of the human mind have probably never attained such force and keenness, the proof of what society can do for the individual has never been so strikingly exhibited, as among the small groups of men who possessed civil privileges in the small republics of antiquity. The whole framework of our political ideas, to say nothing of our philosophy, is derived from them. But in them this extraordinary efflorescence of the privileged class was accompanied by the slavery of the multitude. That slavery was the condition on which it depended, and for that reason it was doomed to decay. There is no clearer ordinance of that supreme reason, often dark to us, which governs the course of man's affairs, than that no body of men should in the long run be able to strengthen itself at the cost of others' weakness. The civilisation and freedom of the ancient world were shortlived because they were partial and exceptional. If the ideal of true freedom is the maximum of power for all members of human society alike to make the best of themselves, we are right in refusing to ascribe the glory of freedom to a state in which the apparent elevation of the few is founded on the degradation of the many, and in ranking modern society, founded as it is on free industry, with all its confusion and ignorant licence and waste of effort, above the most splendid of ancient republics.

If I have given a true account of that freedom which forms the goal of social effort, we shall see that freedom of contract, freedom in all the forms of doing what one will with one's own, is valuable only as a means to an end. That end is what I call freedom in the positive sense: in other words, the liberation of the powers of all men equally for contributions to a common good. No one has a right to do what he will with his own in such a way as to contravene this end. It is only through the guarantee which society gives him that he has property at all, or, strictly speaking, any right to his possessions. This guarantee is founded on a sense of common interest. Every one has an interest in securing to every one else the free use and enjoyment and disposal of his possessions, so long as that freedom on the part of one does not interfere with a like freedom on the part of others, because such freedom contributes to that equal development of the faculties of all which is the highest good for all. This is the true and the only justification of rights of property. Rights of property, however, have been and are claimed which cannot be thus justified. We are all now agreed that men cannot rightly be the property of men. The institution of property being only justifiable as a means to the free exercise of the social capabilities of all, there can be no true right to property of a kind which debars one class of men from such free exercise altogether. We condemn slavery no less when it arises out of a voluntary agreement on the part of the enslaved person. A contract by which any one agreed for a certain consideration to become the slave of another we should reckon a void contract. Here, then, is a limitation upon freedom of contract which we all recognise as rightful. No contract is valid in which human persons, willingly or unwillingly, are dealt with as commodities, because such contracts of necessity defeat the end for which alone society enforces contracts at all.

Are there no other contracts which, less obviously perhaps but really, are open to the same objection? In the first place, let us consider contracts affecting labour. Labour, the economist tells us, is a commodity exchangeable like other commodities. This is in a certain sense true, but it is a commodity which attaches in a peculiar manner to the person of man.

Hence restrictions may need to be placed on the sale of this commodity which would be unnecessary in other cases, in order to prevent labour from being sold under conditions which make it impossible for the person selling it ever to become a free contributor to social good in any form. This is most plainly the case when a man bargains to work under conditions fatal to health, *e.g.* in an unventilated factory. Every injury to the health of the individual is, so far as it goes, a public injury. It is an impediment to the general freedom; so much deduction from our power, as members of society, to make the best of ourselves. Society is, therefore, plainly within its right when it limits freedom of contract for the sale of labour, so far as is done by our laws for the sanitary regulations of factories, workshops, and mines. It is equally within its right in prohibiting the labour of women and young persons beyond certain hours. If they work beyond those hours, the result is demonstrably physical deterioration; which, as demonstrably, carries with it a lowering of the moral forces of society. For the sake of that general freedom of its members to make the best of themselves, which it is the object of civil society to secure, a prohibition should be put by law, which is the deliberate voice of society, on all such contracts of service as in a general way yield such a result. The purchase or hire of unwholesome dwellings is properly forbidden on the same principle. Its application to compulsory education may not be quite so obvious, but it will appear on a little reflection. Without a command of certain elementary arts and knowledge, the individual in modern society is as effectually crippled as by the loss of a limb or a broken constitution. He is not free to develop his faculties. With a view to securing such freedom among its members it is as certainly within the prov-

ince of the state to prevent children from growing up
in that kind of ignorance which practically excludes
them from a free career in life, as it is within its
province to require the sort of building and drainage
necessary for public health.

Our modern legislation then with reference to labour, and education, and health, involving as it does
manifold interference with freedom of contract, is
justified on the ground that it is the business of the
state, not indeed directly to promote moral goodness,
for that, from the very nature of moral goodness, it
cannot do, but to maintain the conditions without
which a free exercise of the human faculties is impossible. It does not indeed follow that it is advisable for the state to do all which it is justified in doing.
We are often warned nowadays against the danger
of over-legislation; or, as I heard it put in a speech
of the present home secretary[12] in days when he was
sowing his political wild oats, of 'grandmotherly government.' There may be good ground for the warn-
ing, but at any rate we should be quite clear what we
mean by it. The outcry against state interference is
often raised by men whose real objection is not to
state interference but to centralisation, to the constant
aggression of the central executive upon local authorities. As I have already pointed out, compulsion at
the discretion of some elected municipal board proceeds just as much from the state as does compulsion
exercised by a government office in London. No
doubt, much needless friction is avoided, much is
gained in the way of elasticity and adjustment to circumstances, by the independent local administration
of general laws; and most of us would agree that of

---

[12] *The present Home Secretary:* Sir William Harcourt (1827-
1904), Liberal member of Parliament for Oxford, later a leader
of the Liberal Party after Gladstone's death.

late there has been a dangerous tendency to override municipal discretion by the hard and fast rules of London 'departments.' But centralisation is one thing: over-legislation, or the improper exercise of the power of the state, quite another. It is one question whether of late the central government has been unduly trenching on local government, and another question whether the law of the state, either as administered by central or by provincial authorities, has been unduly interfering with the discretion of individuals. We may object most strongly to advancing centralisation, and yet wish that the law should put rather more than less restraint on those liberties of the individual which are a social nuisance. But there are some political speculators whose objection is not merely to centralisation, but to the extended action of law altogether. They think that the individual ought to be left much more to himself than has of late been the case. Might not our people, they ask, have been trusted to learn in time for themselves to eschew unhealthy dwellings, to refuse dangerous and degrading employment, to get their children the schooling necessary for making their way in the world? Would they not for their own comfort, if not from more chivalrous feeling, keep their wives and daughters from overwork? Or, failing this, ought not women, like men, to learn to protect themselves? Might not all the rules, in short, which legislation of the kind we have been discussing is intended to attain, have been attained without it; not so quickly, perhaps, but without tampering so dangerously with the independence and self-reliance of the people?

Now, we shall probably all agree that a society in which the public health was duly protected, and necessary education duly provided for, by the spontaneous action of individuals, was in a higher condition

than one in which the compulsion of law was needed
to secure these ends. But we must take men as we
find them. Until such a condition of society is
reached, it is the business of the state to take the
best security it can for the young citizens' growing up
in such health and with so much knowledge as is
necessary for their real freedom. In so doing it need
not at all interfere with the independence and self-
reliance of those whom it requires to do what they
would otherwise do for themselves. The man who,
of his own right feeling, saves his wife from overwork
and sends his children to school, suffers no moral degradation from a law which, if he did not do this for
himself, would seek to make him do it. Such a man
does not feel the law as constraint at all. To him it is
simply a powerful friend. It gives him security for
that being done efficiently which, with the best
wishes, he might have much trouble in getting done
efficiently if left to himself. No doubt it relieves him
from some of the responsibility which would otherwise fall to him as head of a family, but, if he is what
we are supposing him to be, in proportion as he is
relieved of responsibilities in one direction he will
assume them in another. The security which the
state gives him for the safe housing and sufficient
schooling of his family will only make him the more
careful for their well-being in other respects, which
he is left to look after for himself. We need have no
fear, then, of such legislation having an ill effect on
those who, without the law, would have seen to that
being done, though probably less efficiently, which
the law requires to be done. But it was not their
case that the laws we are considering were especially
meant to meet. It was the overworked women, the
ill-housed and untaught families, for whose benefit
they were intended. And the question is whether

without these laws the suffering classes could have been delivered quickly or slowly from the condition they were in. Could the enlightened self-interest or benevolence of individuals, working under a system of unlimited freedom of contract, have ever brought them into a state compatible with the free development of the human faculties? No one considering the facts can have any doubt as to the answer to this question. Left to itself, or to the operation of casual benevolence, a degraded population perpetuates and increases itself. Read any of the authorised accounts, given before royal or parliamentary commissions, of the state of the labourers, especially of the women and children, as they were in our great industries before the law was first brought to bear on them, and before freedom of contract was first interfered with in them. Ask yourself what chance there was of a generation, born and bred under such conditions, ever contracting itself out of them. Given a certain standard of moral and material well-being, people may be trusted not to sell their labour, or the labour of their children, on terms which would not allow that standard to be maintained. But with large masses of our population, until the laws we have been considering took effect, there was no such standard. There was nothing on their part, in the way either of self-respect or established demand for comforts, to prevent them from working and living, or from putting their children to work and live, in a way in which no one who is to be a healthy and free citizen can work and live. No doubt there were many high-minded employers who did their best for their workpeople before the days of state-interference, but they could not prevent less scrupulous hirers of labour from hiring it on the cheapest terms. It is true that cheap labour is in the long run dear labour, but it is so only in the long run, and eager traders do not think of the long run. If labour is to be had under conditions incompatible with the health or decent housing or education of the labourer, there will always be plenty of people to buy it under those conditions, careless of the burden in the shape of rates and taxes which they may be laying up for posterity. Either the standard of well-being on the part of the sellers of labour must prevent them from selling their labour under those conditions, or the law must prevent it. With a population such as ours was forty years ago, and still largely is, the law must prevent it and continue the prevention for some generations, before the sellers will be in a state to prevent it for themselves.

As there is practically no danger of a reversal of our factory and school laws, it may seem needless to dwell at such length on their justification. I do so for two reasons; partly to remind the younger generation of citizens of the great blessing which they inherited in those laws, and of the interest which they still have in their completion and extension; but still more in order to obtain some clear principles for our guidance when we approach those difficult questions of the immediate future, the questions of the land law and the liquor law.

I pointed out just now that, though labour might be reckoned an exchangeable commodity, it differed from all other commodities, inasmuch as it was inseparable from the person of the labourer. Land, too, has its characteristics, which distinguish it from ordinary commodities. It is from the land, or through the land, that the raw material of all wealth is obtained. It is only upon the land that we can live; only across the land that we can move from place to place. The state, therefore, in the interest of that public freedom which it is its business to maintain, cannot allow the individual to deal as he likes with his land to the same extent to which it allows him to deal as he likes with other commodities. It is an established principle, *e.g.* that the sale of land should be enforced by law when public convenience requires it. The land-owner of course gets the full value, often much more than the full value, of the land which he is compelled to sell, but of no ordinary commodity is the sale thus enforced at all. This illustrates the peculiar necessity in the public interest of putting some restraint on a man's liberty of doing what he will with his own, when it is land that he calls his own. The question is whether in the same interest further restraint does not need to be imposed on the liberty of the land-owner than is at present the case. Should not the state, which for public purposes compels the sale of land, also for public purposes prevent it from being tied up in a manner which prevents its natural distribution and keeps it in the hands of those who cannot make the most of it? At the present the greater part of the land of England is held under settlements which prevent the nominal owner from either dividing his land among his children or from selling any part of it for their benefit. It is so settled that all of it necessarily goes to the owner's eldest son. So far as any sale is allowed it must only be for the benefit of that favoured son. The evil effects of this system are twofold. In the first place it almost entirely prevents the sale of agricultural land in small quantities, and thus hinders the formation of that mainstay of social order and contentment, a class of small proprietors tilling their own land. Secondly it keeps large quantities of land in the hands of men who are too much burdened by debts or family charges to improve it. The landlord in such cases has not the money to improve, the tenant has not the security which would justify him in improving. Thus a great part of the land of England is left in a state in which, according to such eminent and impartial authorities as lord Derby and lord Leicester,[13] it does not yield half of what it might. Now what is the remedy for this evil? Various palliative measures have been suggested. A very elaborate one was introduced by lord Cairns[14] a year ago, but it fell short of the only sufficient remedy. It did not propose to prevent landlords for the future from making settlements of the kind described. It left the old power of settling land untouched, on the ground that to interfere with it would be to prevent the landlord from doing what he would with his own. We urge on the contrary that this particular power on the part of the landlord of dealing with his property, imposing, as it does, the weight of the dead hand on posterity, is against the public interest. On the simple and recognised principle that no man's land is his own for purposes incompatible with the public convenience, we ask that legal sanction should be withheld for the future from settlements which thus interfere with the distribution and improvement of land.

Such a change, though it would limit in one direction the power of dealing with land, would extend it in other directions. It would render English land on the whole a much more marketable commodity than it is at present. Its effect would be to restrain the owner of land in any one generation from putting

[13] *Lord Derby:* Edward Henry Stanley (1826-93), 15th Earl of Derby, son of the former Prime Minister, Foreign Secretary twice in Conservative Governments, then became a Liberal. *Lord Leicester:* Thomas Wm. Coke (1822-1909), 2nd Earl of Leicester, prominent Whig agriculturist.

[14] *Lord Cairns:* Hugh McC. Cairns (1819-85), 1st Earl Cairns, prominent lawyer and Conservative politician, Lord Chancellor under Disraeli in 1868 and 1874-80.

restraints on the disposal of it in succeeding generations. It would, therefore, have the support of those
liberals who are most jealous of any interference with
freedom of contract. When we come to the relations between landlord and tenant, we are on more
difficult ground. It is agreed that as a general rule
the more freedom of contract we have the better, with
a view to that more positive freedom which consists
in an open field for all men to make the best of themselves. But we must not sacrifice the end to the
means. If there are certain kinds of contract for the
use of land which interfere seriously with the public
convenience, but which the parties immediately concerned cannot be trusted to abstain from in their own
interest, such contracts should be invalid by law. It
is on this ground that we justify the prohibition by
the act of last session of agreements between landlord
and tenant which reserve the ground game to the
landlord. If the farmers only had been concerned
in the matter, they might perhaps have been left to
take care of themselves. But there were public interests at stake. The country cannot afford the waste of
produce and discouragement of good husbandry
which result from excessive game-preserving; nor can
it rightly allow that widespread temptation to lawless
habits which arises from a sort of half and half property being scattered over the country without any
possibility of its being sufficiently protected. The
agreements in question, therefore, were against the
public interest, and as the tenant farmers themselves,
from long habits of dependence, could not be trusted
to refuse them, there was no alternative but to render
them illegal. Perhaps as we become more alive to the
evil which the ground game act but partially remedied, we shall demand further legislation in the same
direction, and insist that some limit be put, not merely

to the landlord's power of reserving the game on land let to farmers, but to his power of keeping land out of cultivation or turning it into forest for the sake of his amusement.

But while admitting that in this matter of game, from long habit of domination on one side and dependence on the other, landlord and farmer could not safely be left to voluntary agreements, and that a special law was needed to break the back of a mischievous practice, are we to allow that in the public interest the English farmer generally needs to be restrained by law from agreements with his landlord, into which he might be induced to enter if left to himself? Is he not sufficiently enlightened as to his own interest, which is also the interest of the public, and sufficiently free in maintaining it, to refuse to take land except on conditions which will enable him to make the best of it? We may wish that he were, we may hope that some day he will be, but facts show that at present he is not. The great majority of English farmers hold their farms under the liability to be turned out without compensation at six months' or a year's notice. Now it is certain that land cannot be farmed as the public interest requires that is should be, except by an expenditure of capital on the part of the farmers, which will not, as a general rule, be risked so long as he holds his land on these terms. It is true that, under a good landlord, the yearly tenant is as secure as if he held a long lease. But all landlords are not good, nor is a good landlord immortal. He may have a spendthrift eldest son, from whom under his settlement he cannot withhold the estate, and upon whose accession to the estate the temporary security previously enjoyed by yearly tenants will disappear. Whatever the reason, the fact remains that yearly tenancy under the present law is not sufficient to secure a due application of capital to the soil. "The best agriculture is found on farms where tenants are protected by leases; the next best on farms where tenants are protected by the 'Lincolnshire custom'; the worst of all on farms whose tenants are not protected at all, but rely on the honour of their landlords";[15] and this latter class of farms covers the greater part of England. Here, then, is proof that the majority of English farmers have either not been intelligent enough, or not independent enough, to insist on those contracts with their landlords which as a rule are necessary for good farming. They may in time become so, but meanwhile, with the daily increasing pressure on the means of subsistence, the country cannot afford to wait. We do not ask for any such change of the law as would hinder or discourage the farmer from making voluntary contracts with the landlord for the protection of both parties. We only wish in the public interest, which is the interest of good farming, to prevent him from taking a farm, as he now generally does, on terms incompatible with security in the outlay of capital. In the absence of leases, we wish a sufficient tenant-right to be guaranteed by law, such tenant-right as would secure to the out-going tenant the full value of unexhausted improvements. It is only thus, we believe, that we can bring about that due cultivation of the soil which is every day becoming of greater importance to our crowded population.

This protection, which is all that can reasonably be asked for the English farmer, falls far short of that which the most impartial judges believe to be necessary for the peasant farmers in Ireland. The differ-

[15] [Note by Green] Quoted from *English Land and English Landlords,* by the Hon. G. C. Brodrick; Cassell & Co. [London], 1881.

ence between the farmers of the Irish counties may
be briefly stated thus. In Ireland, far more frequently than in England, the tenant is practically
not a free agent in the contract he makes with his
landlord. In England, during the last two or three
years, the landlord has often been more afraid of
losing the tenant than the tenant of losing his farm.
It is comparatively easy for a man who does not suc-
ceed in getting a farm on terms under which he can
make it pay, to get a living in other ways. Thus in
England a farmer is seldom under such pressure as
to be unable to make a bargain with a landlord which
shall be reasonably to his own advantage. In Ireland
it is otherwise. The farmers there are relatively far
more numerous, and, as a rule, far poorer. Nearly
three-fourths of the Irish farmers (423,000 out of
596,000) hold less than thirty acres apiece; nearly half
of them hold under fifteen acres. A tenant on that
small scale is in a very different position for bargaining with a landlord from the English farmer, as we
commonly know him, with his 200 acres or more.
Apart from his little farm the tenant has nothing to
turn his hand to. With the exception of the linen-
making in the north, Ireland has no industry but agriculture out of which a living can be made. It has
been said on good authority that in many parts of Ireland eviction means starvation to the evicted tenant.
This may be a strong statement, but there is no doubt
that to an Irishman of the south and west (the districts
at present disturbed) the hiring of land to till presents itself as a necessity of life. The only alternative
is emigration, and during the recent years of depression in America that alternative was to a great extent closed. Hence an excessive competition for
farms, and a readiness on the part of the smaller ten-

ants to put up with any enhancement of rent rather than relinquish their holdings. Under such conditions freedom of contract is little more than a name. The peasant farmer is scarcely more free to contract with his landlord than is a starving labourer to bargain for good wages with a master who offers him work. When many contracts between landlord and tenants are made under such pressure, reverence for contract, which is the safeguard of society, is sure to disappear, and this I believe to be the chief reason why the farmers of southern and western Ireland have been so easily led astray by the agitation of the land league.[16] That agitation strikes at the roots of all contract, and therefore at the very foundation of modern society; but if we would effectually withstand it, we must cease to insist on maintaining the forms of free contract where the reality is impossible. We must in some way give the farmers of Ireland by law that protection which, as a rule, they have been too weak to obtain for themselves singly by contract, protection against the confiscation of the fruits of the labour and money they have spent on the soil, whether that confiscation take the form of actual eviction or of a constant enhancement of rent. To uphold the sanctity of contracts is doubtless a prime business of government, but it is no less its business to provide against contracts being made, which, from the helplessness of one

[16] *Land League:* the Irish National Land League, which agitated against 'landlordism' with the slogan "the land for the people" during the near-famine years of 1879-81. Its tactics included withholding payment of rents, resisting evictions, and boycotting; sporadic acts of violence, including some cases of murder, occurred in the course of the agitation. The Irish Land Act passed by Gladstone's Government in August 1881, some months after Green's lecture, aimed at allaying the discontent in Ireland; it achieved partial success. (See N. D. Palmer, *The Irish Land League Crisis,* New Haven, 1940.)

of the parties to them, instead of being a security for freedom, become an instrument of disguised oppression.

I have left myself little time to speak of the principles on which some of us hold that, in the matter of intoxicating drinks, a further limitation of freedom of contract is needed in the interest of general freedom. I say a further limitation, because there is no such thing as a free sale of these drinks at present. Men are not at liberty to buy and sell them when they will, where they will, and as they will. But our present licensing system, while it creates a class of monopolists especially interested in resisting any effectual restraint of the liquor traffic, does little to lessen the facilities for obtaining strong drink. Indeed the principle upon which licences have been generally given has been avowedly to make it easy to get drink. The restriction of the hours of sale is no doubt a real check so far as it goes, but it remains the case that every one who has a weakness for drink has the temptation staring him in the face during all hours but those when he ought to be in bed. The effect of the present system, in short, is to prevent the drink-shops from coming unpleasantly near the houses of well-to-do people, and to crowd them upon the quarters occupied by the poorer classes, who have practically no power of keeping the nuisance from them. Now it is clear that the only remedy which the law can afford for this state of things must take the form either of more stringent rules of licensing, or of a power entrusted to the householders in each district of excluding the sale of intoxicants altogether from among them.

I do not propose to discuss the comparative merits of these methods of procedure. One does not exclude the other. They may very well be combined. One may be best suited for one kind of population, the other for another kind. But either, to be effectual, must involve a large interference with the liberty of the individual to do as he likes in the matter of buying and selling alcohol. It is the justifiability of that interference that I wish briefly to consider.

We justify it on the simple ground of the recognised right on the part of society to prevent men from doing as they like, if, in the exercise of their peculiar tastes in doing as they like, they create a social nuisance. There is no right to freedom in the purchase and sale of a particular commodity, if the general result of allowing such freedom is to detract from freedom in the higher sense, from the general power of men to make the best of themselves. Now with anyone who looks calmly at the facts, there can be no doubt that the present habits of drinking in England do lay a heavy burden on the free development of man's powers for social good, a heavier burden probably than arises from all other preventible causes put together. It used to be the fashion to look on drunkenness as a vice which was the concern only of the person who fell into it, so long as it did not lead him to commit an assault on his neighbours. No thoughtful man any longer looks on it in this way. We know that, however decently carried on, the excessive drinking of one man means an injury to others in health, purse, and capability, to which no limits can be placed. Drunkenness in the head of a family means, as a rule, the impoverishment and degradation of all members of the family; and the presence of a drink-shop at the corner of a street means, as a rule, the drunkenness of a certain number of heads of families in that street. Remove the drink-shops, and, as the experience of many happy communities sufficiently shows, you almost, perhaps in time altogether, remove the drunkenness. Here, then, is a wide-spreading social evil, of which society may, if it will, by a restraining law, to a great extent, rid itself, to the infinite enhancement of the positive freedom enjoyed by its members. All that is required for the attainment of so blessed a result is so much effort and self-sacrifice on the part of the majority of citizens as is necessary for the enactment and enforcement of the restraining law. The majority of citizens may still be far from prepared for such an effort. That is a point on which I express no opinion. To attempt a restraining law in advance of the social sentiment necessary to give real effect to it, is always a mistake. But to argue that an effectual law in restraint of the drink-traffic would be a wrongful interference with individual liberty, is to ignore the essential condition under which alone every particular liberty can rightly be allowed to the individual, the condition, namely, that the allowance of that liberty is not, as a rule, and on the whole, an impediment to social good.

The more reasonable opponents of the restraint for which I plead, would probably argue not so much that it was necessarily wrong in principle, as that it was one of those short cuts to a good end which ultimately defeat their own object. They would take the same line that has been taken by the opponents of state-interference in all its forms. 'Leave the people to themselves,' they would say; 'as their standard of self-respect rises, as they become better housed and better educated, they will gradually shake off the evil habit. The cure so effected may not be so rapid as that brought by a repressive law, but it will be more lasting. Better that it should come more slowly through the spontaneous action of individuals, than more quickly through compulsion.'

But here again we reply that it is dangerous to wait.

The slower remedy might be preferable if we were sure that it was a remedy at all, but we have no such assurance. There is strong reason to think the contrary. Every year that the evil is left to itself, it becomes greater. The vested interest in the encouragement of the vice becomes larger, and the persons affected by it more numerous. If any abatement of it has already taken place, we may fairly argue that this is because it has not been altogether left to itself; for the licensing law, as it is, is much more stringent and more stringently administered than it was ten years ago. A drunken population naturally perpetuates and increases itself. Many families, it is true, keep emerging from the conditions which render them specially liable to the evil habit, but on the other hand descent through drunkenness from respectability to squalor is constantly going on. The families of drunkards do not seem to be smaller than those of sober men, though they are shorter-lived; and that the children of a drunkard should escape from drunkenness is what we call almost a miracle. Better education, better housing, more healthy rules of labour, no doubt lessen the temptations to drink for those who have the benefit of these advantages, but meanwhile drunkenness is constantly recruiting the ranks of those who cannot be really educated, who will not be better housed, who make their employments dangerous and unhealthy. An effectual liquor law in short is the necessary complement of our factory acts, our education acts, our public health acts. Without it the full measure of their usefulness will never be attained. They were all opposed in their turn by the same arguments that are now used against a restraint of the facilities for drinking. Sometimes it was the argument that the state had no business to interfere with the liberties of the individual. Sometimes it was the dilatory plea that the better nature of man would in time assert itself, and that meanwhile it would be lowered by compulsion. Happily a sense of the facts and necessities of the case got the better of the delusive cry of liberty. Act after act was passed preventing master and workman, parent and child, housebuilder and householder, from doing as they pleased, with the result of a great addition to the real freedom of society. The spirit of self-reliance and independence was not weakened by those acts. Rather it received a new development. The dead weight of ignorance and unhealthy surroundings, with which it would otherwise have had to struggle, being partially removed by law, it was more free to exert itself for higher objects. When we ask for a stringent liquor law, which should even go to the length of allowing the householders of a district to exclude the drink traffic altogether, we are only asking for a continuation of the same work, a continuation necessary to its complete success. It is a poor sophistry to tell us that it is moral corwardice to seek to remove by law a temptation which every one ought to be able to resist for himself. It is not the part of a considerate self-reliance to remain in presence of a temptation merely for the sake of being tempted. When all temptations are removed which law can remove, there will still be room enough, nay, much more room, for the play of our moral energies. The temptation to excessive drinking is one which upon sufficient evidence we hold that the law can at least greatly diminish. If it can, it ought to do so. This then, along with the effectual liberation of the soil, is the next great conquest which our democracy, on behalf of its own true freedom, has to make. The danger of legislation, either in the interests of a privileged class or for the promotion of particular religious opinions, we may fairly assume to be over. The popular jealousy of law, once justifiable enough, is therefore out of date. The citizens of England now make its law. We ask them by law to put a restraint on themselves in the matter of strong drink. We ask them further to limit, or even altogether to give up, the not very precious liberty of buying and selling alcohol, in order that they may become more free to exercise the faculties and improve the talents which God has given them.

EDITOR'S NOTE

In Green's usage, the term 'liberal legislation' includes not only legislation passed by the Liberal Party, but also many measures carried by Conservative Governments and by bipartisan majorities. Although some of these measures, like Peel's repeal of the Corn Laws, could reasonably be regarded as 'liberal' in the sense of having been taken over from the prevailing doctrines of 'Liberalism,' the same cannot be said for the factory acts, for example, which owed much to Tory philanthropists like Lord Shaftesbury and were opposed by many Liberals. Ultimately, the term 'liberal legislation' includes any measure that enlarged freedom (liberty). That measures like the factory acts and the proposed Irish Land Act fell into this category was, of course, the point Green was trying to establish. If he seemed to imply a closer connection between 'liberal legislation' and the Liberal Party than appears warranted in retrospect, it should be remembered that he was not so much engaging in historical analysis as attempting to rally Liberal support for liberal legislation.

The term 'freedom of contract' should be understood in a sense wider than the legal concept. The reader may recall the central role that the idea of contract played in Liberal mythology, from Locke's assertion of the 'Social Compact' against Sir Robert Filmer's 'patriarchal' theory of government to Sir Henry Maine's inadvertent summation of the Liberal philosophy of history in the proposition that "the movement of the progressive societies has hitherto been a movement *from Status to Contract.*" (See John Locke, *Two Treatises of Civil Government;* also Maine's *Ancient Law,* London, 1861, end of Chapter V.)   In modern Liberal hands, the idea of contract was turned into a model for social-political relationships: all legitimate authority was grounded on the voluntary consent given by autonomous individuals when they struck a bargain or made an agreement.   The contract model tacitly assumed a society composed of adult males of roughly equal powers; and the early factory acts, by regulating directly only the working conditions of women and children, i.e., the admittedly dependent parts of the population, did not so much conflict with the sanctity of 'freedom of contract' as deal with its exceptions.   The Irish Land Act of 1881, however, regulated the agreements between landowners and tenant-farmers, i.e., between male adults.   For that reason, its prospect provoked great controversy, and its passage was a landmark in the evolution from a *laissez-faire* to a welfare-state pattern of policy.   The Act represented an acknowledgement of the fact that labor and property agreements between adult males of vastly unequal economic power and bargaining position were 'free' only in a formalistic, legal sense: hungry men had to take work or land on whatever terms they could get—unless the government intervened. In the long run, as Arnold Toynbee observed, "The real course of development has been first from status to contract, then from contract to a new kind of status determined by the law,—or, in other words, from unregulated to regulated contract."   (*Lectures on the Industrial Revolution,* London, 1884, page 31.)

THE SENSES OF 'FREEDOM'[1]

1. SINCE in all willing a man is his own object, the will is always free. Or, more properly, a man in willing is necessarily free, since willing constitutes freedom,[2] and 'free will' is the pleonasm 'free freedom.' But while it is important to insist upon this, it is also to be remembered that the nature of the freedom really differs—the freedom means quite different things—according to the nature of the object which the man makes his own, or with which he identifies himself. It is one thing when the object in which self-satisfaction is sought is such as to prevent that self-satisfaction being found, because interfering with the realisation of the seeker's possibilities or his progress towards perfection: it is another thing when it contributes to this end. In the former case the man is a free agent in the act, because through his identification of himself with a certain desired object—through his adoption of it as his good—he makes the motive which determines the act, and is accordingly conscious of himself as its author. But in another sense he is not free, because the objects to which his actions are

---

[1] This selection consists of passages from Green's course of lectures on the "Metaphysic of Ethics" (1879) which were not incorporated into the *Prolegomena to Ethics*. The text printed here is taken from Green's *Works*, Vol. II, pages 308ff. I have abridged Nettleship's cumbersome title, "On the Different Senses of 'Freedom' as Applied to the Will and to the Moral Progress of Man." For related passages, see *Prolegomena to Ethics*, §§97ff.

[2] [Green's note] In that sense in which 'freedom' expresses a state of the soul, as distinct from a civil relation. [See §2.]

directed are objects in which, according to the law of
his being, satisfaction of himself is not to be found.
His will to arrive at self-satisfaction not being adjusted
to the law which determines where this self-satisfaction is to be found, he may be considered in the condition of a bondsman who is carrying out the will of
another, not his own. From this bondage he emerges
into real freedom, not by overcoming the law of his
being, not by getting the better of its necessity,—
every fancied effort to do so is but a new exhibition of
its necessity,—but by making its fulfilment the object
of his will; by seeking the satisfaction of himself in
objects in which he believes it *should be* found, and
seeking it in them *because* he believes it should be
found in them. For the objects so sought, however
various otherwise, have the common characteristic
that, because they are sought in such a spirit, in them
self-satisfaction is to be found; not the satisfaction of
this or that desire, or of each particular desire, but
that satisfaction, otherwise called peace or blessedness, which consists in the whole man having found
his object; which indeed we never experience in its
fulness, which we only approach to fall away from it
again, but of which we know enough to be sure that
we only fail to attain it because we fail to seek it in
the fulfilment of the law of our being, because we have
not brought ourselves to 'gladly do and suffer what we
must.'

To the above statement several objections may be
made. They will chiefly turn on two points; (*a*) the
use made of the term 'freedom'; (*b*) the view that a
man is subject to a law of his being, in virtue of which
he at once seeks self-satisfaction, and is prevented
from finding it in the objects which he actually desires,
and in which he ordinarily seeks it.

2. As to the sense given to 'freedom,' it must of

course be admitted that every usage of the term to express anything but a social and political relation of one man to others involves a metaphor. Even in the original application its sense is by no means fixed. It always implies indeed some exemption from compulsion by others, but the extent and conditions of this exemption, as enjoyed by the 'freeman' in different states of society, are very various. As soon as the term 'freedom' comes to be applied to anything else than an established relation between a man and other men, its sense fluctuates much more. Reflecting on their consciousness, on their 'inner life' (i.e. their life as viewed from within), men apply to it the terms with which they are familiar as expressing their relations to each other. In virtue of that power of self-distinction and self-objectification, which he expresses whenever he says 'I,' a man can set over against himself his whole nature or any of its elements, and apply to the relation thus established in thought a term borrowed from relations of outward life. Hence, as in Plato, the terms 'freedom' and 'bondage' may be used to express a relation between the man on the one side, as distinguishing himself from all impulses that do not tend to his true good, and those impulses on the other. He is a 'slave' when they are masters of him, 'free' when master of them. The metaphor in this form was made further use of by the Stoics, and carried on into the doctrines of the Christian Church. Since there is no kind of impulse or interest which a man cannot so distinguish from himself as to present it as an alien power, of which the influence on him is bondage, the particular application of the metaphor is quite arbitrary. It may come to be thought that the only freedom is to be found in a life of absolute detachment from all interests; a life in which the pure ego converses solely with itself or with a God, who is the

same abstraction under another name. This is a view
into which both saints and philosophers have been apt
to fall. It means practically, so far as it means anything, absorption in some one interest with which the
man identifies himself in exclusion of all other interests, which he sets over against himself as an influence
to be kept aloof.

With St. Paul the application of the metaphor has
a special character of its own. With him 'freedom' is
specially freedom from the law, from ordinances, from
the fear which these inspire,—a freedom which is attained through the communication of what he calls
the 'spirit of adoption' or 'sonship.' The law, merely
as law or as an external command, is a source of bondage in a double sense. Presenting to man a command
which yet it does not give him power to obey, it
destroys the freedom of the life in which he does
what he likes without recognising any reason why he
should not (the state of which St. Paul says 'I was alive
without the law once'); it thus puts him in bondage to
fear, and at the same time, exciting a wish for obedience to itself which other desires (φρόνημα σαρκός)[3]
prevent from being accomplished, it makes the man
feel the bondage of the flesh. 'What I will, that I do
not'; there is a power, the flesh, of which I am the
slave, and which prevents me from performing my
will to obey the law. Freedom (also called 'peace,'
and 'reconciliation') comes when the spirit expressed
in the law (for the law is itself 'spiritual' according to
St. Paul; the 'flesh' through which it is weak is mine,
not the law's) becomes the principle of action in the
man. To the man thus delivered, as St. Paul conceives him, we might almost apply phraseology like
Kant's. 'He is free because conscious of himself as
the author of the law which he obeys.' He is no

[3] *Phronema sarkos*: desires of the flesh.

longer a servant, but a son. He is conscious of union with God, whose will as an external law he before sought in vain to obey, but whose 'righteousness is fulfilled' in him now that he 'walks after the spirit.' What was before 'a law of sin and death' is now a 'law of the spirit of life.' (See *Epistle to the Romans*, viii.)

3. But though there is a point of connection between St. Paul's conception of freedom and bondage and that of Kant, which renders the above phrase applicable in a certain sense to the 'spiritual man' of St. Paul, yet the two conceptions are very different. Moral bondage with Kant, as with Plato and the Stoics, is bondage to the flesh. The heteronomy[4] of the will is its submission to the impulse of pleasure-seeking, as that of which man is not in respect of his reason the author, but which belongs to him as a merely natural being. A state of bondage to law, as such, he does not contemplate. It might even be urged that Kant's 'freedom' or 'autonomy' of the will, in the only sense in which he supposed it attainable by man, is very much like the state described by St. Paul as that from which the communication of the spirit brings deliverance,— the state in which 'I delight in the law of God after the inward man, but find another law in my members warring with the law of my reason and bringing me into captivity to the law of sin in my members.' For Kant seems to hold that the will is actually 'autonomous,' i.e. determined by pure consciousness of what should be, only in rare acts of the best man. He argues rather for our being conscious of the possibility of such determination, as evidence of an ideal of what

---

[4] *Heteronomy of the will:* subjection of the rational will to something outside itself. Cf. *autonomy:* obedience of the rational will to its own laws. (See Kant's *Critique of Practical Reason.*)

the good will is, than for the fact that anyone is actually so determined. And every determination of the will that does not proceed from pure consciousness of what should be he ascribes to the pleasure-seeking which belongs to man merely as a 'Natur-wesen,'[5] or as St. Paul might say 'to the law of sin in his members.' What, it may be asked, is such 'freedom,' or rather such consciousness of the possibility of freedom, worth? May we not apply to it St. Paul's words, 'By the law is the knowledge of sin'? The practical result to the individual of that consciousness of the possibility of freedom which is all that the autonomy of will, as really attainable by man, according to Kant's view, amounts to, is to make him aware of the heteronomy of his will, of its bondage to motives of which reason is not the author.

4. This is an objection which many of Kant's statements of his doctrine, at any rate, fairly challenge. It was chiefly because he seemed to make freedom[6] an unrealised and unrealisable state, that his moral doctrine was found unsatisfactory by Hegel. Hegel holds that freedom, as the condition in which the will is determined by an object adequate to itself, or by an object which itself as reason constitutes, is realised in the state. He thinks of the state in a way not familiar to Englishmen, a way not unlike that in which Greek philosophers thought of the πόλις,[7] as a society governed by laws and institutions and established customs which secure the common good of the members of the

---

[5] *Natur-wesen:* natural (*vs.* spiritual) being, animal.

[6] [Green's note] In the sense of 'autonomy of the rational will,' or determination by an object which reason constitutes, as distinct from determination by an object which the man makes his own; this latter determination Kant would have recognized as characteristic of every human act, properly so called.

[7] See note 11, below.

society—enable them to make the best of themselves
—and are recognised as doing so. Such a state is
'objective freedom'; freedom is realised in it because
in it the reason, the self-determining principle operat-
ing in man as his will, has found a perfect expression
for itself (as an artist may be considered to express
himself in a perfect work of art); and the man who is
determined by the objects which the well-ordered
state presents to him is determined by that which is
the perfect expression of his reason, and is thus free.

5. There is, no doubt, truth in this view. I have
already tried to show[8] how the self-distinguishing and
self-seeking consciousness of man, acting in and upon
those human wants and ties and affections which in
their proper human character have as little reality
apart from it as it apart from them, gives rise to a system of social relations, with laws, customs, and institutions corresponding; and how in this system the individual's consciousness of the absolutely desirable, of
something that should be, of an ideal to be realised
in his life, finds a content or object which has been
constituted or brought into being by that consciousness itself as working through generations of men;
how interests are thus supplied to the man of a more
concrete kind than the interest in fulfilment of a universally binding law because universally binding, but
which yet are the product of reason, and in satisfying
which he is conscious of attaining a true good, a good
contributory to the perfection of himself and his kind.
There is thus something in all forms of society that
tends to the freedom[9] at least of some favoured individuals, because it tends to actualise in them the
possibility of that determination by objects conceived

[8] In earlier lectures. (See *Prolegomena to Ethics*, esp.
§§199ff.)

[9] [Green's note] In the sense of 'autonomy of the will.'

as desirable in distinction from objects momentarily desired, which is determination by reason.[10] To put it otherwise, the effect of his social relations on a man thus favoured is that, whereas in all willing the individual seeks to satisfy himself, this man seeks to satisfy himself, not as one who feels this or that desire, but as one who conceives, whose nature demands, a permanent good. So far as it is thus in respect of his rational nature that he makes himself an object to himself, his will is autonomous. This was the good which the ideal πόλις, as conceived by the Greek philosophers, secured for the true πολίτης, the man who, entering into the idea of the πόλις, was equally qualified ἄρχειν καὶ ἄρχεσθαι.[11] No doubt in the actual Greek πόλις there was some tendency in this direction, some tendency to rationalise and moralise the citizen. Without the real tendency the ideal possibility would not have suggested itself. And in more primitive forms of society, so far as they were based on family or tribal relations, we can see that the same tendency must have been at work, just as in modern life the consciousness of his position as member or head of a family, wherever it exists, necessarily does something to moralise a man. In modern Christendom, with the extension of citizenship, the security of family life to all men (so far as law and police can secure it), the establishment in various forms of Christian fellowship of which the moralising functions grow as those of the magistrate diminish, the number of individuals whom society awakens to interests in objects contributory to human perfection tends to increase. So far the modern state, in that full sense in which Hegel uses the term (as including all the agencies for common good

[10] [Nettleship's note] The last clause is queried in the MS.
[11] *Polis:* city-state. *Polites:* citizen. *Archein kai archesthai:* to rule and be ruled. (See Aristotle's *Politics.*)

of a law-abiding people), does contribute to the realisation of freedom, if by freedom we understand the autonomy of the will or its determination by rational objects, objects which help to satisfy the demand of reason, the effort after self-perfection.

6. On the other hand, it would seem that we cannot significantly speak of freedom except with reference to individual persons; that only in them can freedom be realised; that therefore the realisation of freedom in the state can only mean the attainment of freedom by individuals through influences which the state (in the wide sense spoken of) supplies,—'freedom' here, as before, meaning not the mere self-determination which renders us responsible, but determination by reason, 'autonomy of the will'; and that under the best conditions of any society that has ever been such realisation of freedom is most imperfect. To an Athenian slave, who might be used to gratify a master's lust, it would have been a mockery to speak of the state as a realisation of freedom; and perhaps it would not be much less so to speak of it as such to an untaught and underfed denizen of a London yard with gin-shops on the right hand and on the left. What Hegel says of the state in this respect seems as hard to square with facts as what St. Paul says of the Christian whom the manifestation of Christ has transferred from bondage into 'the glorious liberty of the sons of God.' In both cases the difference between the ideal and the actual seems to be ignored, and tendencies seem to be spoken of as if they were accomplished facts. It is noticeable that by uncritical readers of St. Paul the account of himself as under the law (in *Romans* vii.), with the 'law of sin in his members warring against the law of his reason,' is taken as applicable to the regenerate Christian, though evidently St. Paul meant it as a description of the state from which the Gospel, the 'mani-

festation of the Son of God in the likeness of sinful flesh,' set him free. They are driven to this interpretation because, though they can understand St. Paul's account of his deliverance as an account of a deliverance achieved for them but not in them, or as an assurance of what is to be, they cannot adjust it to the actual experience of the Christian life. In the same way Hegel's account of freedom as realised in the state does not seem to correspond to the facts of society as it is, or even as, under the unalterable conditions of human nature, it ever could be; though undoubtedly there is a work of moral liberation, which society, through its various agencies, is constantly carrying on for the individual.

7. Meanwhile it must be borne in mind that in all these different views as to the manner and degree in which freedom is to be attained, 'freedom' does not mean that the man or will is undetermined, nor yet does it mean mere self-determination, which (unless denied altogether, as by those who take the strictly naturalistic view of human action) must be ascribed equally to the man whose will is heteronomous or vicious, and to him whose will is autonomous; equally to the man who recognises the authority of law in what St. Paul would count the condition of a bondman, and to him who fulfils the righteousness of the law in the spirit of adoption. It means a particular kind of self-determination; the state of the man who lives indeed for himself, but for the fulfilment of himself as a 'giver of law universal' (Kant); who lives for himself, but only according to the true idea of himself, according to the law of his being, 'according to nature' (the Stoics); who is so taken up into God, to whom God so gives the spirit, that there is no constraint in his obedience to the divine will (St. Paul); whose interests, as a loyal citizen, are those of a well-ordered state

in which practical reason expresses itself (Hegel). Now none of these modes of self-determination is at all implied in 'freedom' according to the primary meaning of the term, as expressing that relation between one man and others in which he is secured from compulsion. All that is so implied is that a man should have power to do what he wills or prefers. No reference is made to the nature of the will or preference, of the object willed or preferred; whereas according to the usage of 'freedom' in the doctrines we have just been considering, it is not constituted by the mere fact of acting upon preference, but depends wholly on the nature of the preference, upon the kind of object willed or preferred.

8. If it were ever reasonable to wish that the usage of words had been other than it has been (any more than that the processes of nature were other than they are), one might be inclined to wish that the term 'freedom' had been confined to the juristic sense of the power to 'do what one wills'; for the extension of its meaning seems to have caused much controversy and confusion. But, after all, this extension does but represent various stages of reflection upon the self-distinguishing, self-seeking, self-asserting principle, of which the establishment of freedom, as a relation between man and man, is the expression. The reflecting man is not content with the first announcement which analysis makes as to the inward condition of the free man, viz. that he can do what he likes, that he has the power of acting according to his will or preference. In virtue of the same principle which has led him to assert himself against others, and thus to cause there to be such a thing as (outward) freedom, he distinguishes himself from his preference, and asks how he is related to it, whether he determines it or how it is determined. Is he free to will, as he is free

to act; or, as the act is determined by the preference,
is the preference determined by something else? . . .

[Green goes on to discuss various difficulties in the 'free-
will controversy,' and suggests that "All this [confusion]
is the consequence of asking questions about the relation
between a man and his will in terms only appropriate to
the relation between the man and other men, or to that
between the man and his bodily members or the materials
on which he acts through them." (§11)]

13. The right way out of the difficulty lies in the dis-
cernment that the question whether a man is free to
will, or has power over the determinations of his will,
is a question to which there is no answer, because it
is asked in inappropriate terms; in terms that imply
some agency beyond the will which determines what
the will shall be (as the will itself is an agency beyond
the motions of the muscles which determines what
those motions shall be), and that as to this agency it
may be asked whether it does or does not lie in the
man himself.   In truth there is no such agency beyond
the will and determining how the will shall be determined; not in the man, for the will *is* the self-conscious man; not elsewhere than in the man, not outside him, for the self-conscious man has no outside.
He is not a body in space with other bodies elsewhere
in space acting upon it and determining its motions.
The self-conscious man is determined by objects,
which in order to be objects must already be in consciousness, and in order to be *his* objects, the objects
which determine him, must already have been made
his own.   To say that they have power over him or
his will, and that he or his will has power over them, is
equally misleading.   Such language is only applicable
to the relation between an agent and patient, when
the agent and the patient (or at any rate the agent)

can exist separately. But self-consciousness and its object, will and its object, form a single individual unity. Without the constitutive action of man or his will the objects do not exist; apart from determination by some object neither he nor his will would be more than an unreal abstraction. . . .

15. . . . Throughout the controversy as to free will that has been carried on among British psychologists . . . [t]he freedom, claimed or denied for the will, has been claimed or denied for it irrespectively of those objects willed, on the nature of which the goodness or badness of the will depends.

16. On the other hand, with the Stoics, St. Paul, Kant, and Hegel, as we have seen, the attainment of freedom (at any rate of the reality of freedom, as distinct from some mere possibility of it which constitutes the distinctive human nature) depends on the character of the objects willed. In all these ways of thinking, however variously the proper object of will is conceived, it is only as directed to this object, and thus (in Hegelian language) corresponding to its idea, that the will is supposed to be free. The good will is free, not the bad will. Such a view of course implies some element of identity between good will and bad will, between will as not yet corresponding to its idea and will as so corresponding. . . .

17. Now the propriety or impropriety of the use of 'freedom' to express the state of the will, not as directed to any and every object, but only to those to which, according to the law of nature or the will of God or its 'idea,' it should be directed, is a matter of secondary importance. This usage of the term is, at any rate, no more a departure from the primary or juristic sense than is its application to the will as distinct from action in any sense whatever. And certainly the unsophisticated man, as soon as the usage of 'freedom'

to express exemption from control by other men and ability to do as he likes is departed from, can much more readily assimilate the notion of states of the inner man described as bondage to evil passions, to terrors of the law, or on the other hand as freedom from sin and law, freedom in the consciousness of union with God, or of harmony with the true law of one's being, freedom of true loyalty, freedom in devotion to self-imposed duties, than he can assimilate the notion of freedom as freedom to will anything and everything, or as exemption from determination by motives, or the constitution by himself of the motives which determine his will. And there is so far less to justify the extension of the usage of the term in these latter ways than in the former. It would seem indeed that there is a real community of meaning between 'freedom' as expressing the condition of a citizen of a civilised state, and 'freedom' as expressing the condition of a man who is inwardly 'master of himself.' That is to say, the practical conception by a man ('practical' in the sense of having a tendency to realise itself) of a self-satisfaction to be attained in his becoming what he should be, what he has it in him to be, in fulfilment of the law of his being,—or, to vary the words but not the meaning, in attainment of the righteousness of God, or in perfect obedience to self-imposed law,—this practical conception is the outcome of the same self-seeking principle which appears in a man's assertion of himself against other men and against nature ('against other men,' as claiming their recognition of him as being what they are; 'against nature,' as able to use it). This assertion of himself is the demand for freedom, freedom in the primary or juristic sense of power to act according to choice or preference. So far as such freedom is established for any man, this assertion of himself is made good; and such freedom is precious to him because it is an achievement of the self-seeking principle. It is a first satisfaction of its claims, which is the condition of all other satisfaction of them. The consciousness of it is the first form of self-enjoyment, of the joy of the self-conscious spirit in itself as in the one object of absolute value.

18. This form of self-enjoyment, however, is one which consists essentially in the feeling by the subject of a possibility rather than a reality, of what it has it in itself to become, not of what it actually is. To a captive on first winning his liberty, as to a child in the early experience of power over his limbs and through them over material things, this feeling of a boundless possibility of becoming may give real joy; but gradually the sense of what it is not, of the very little that it amounts to, must predominate over the sense of actual good as attained in it. Thus to the grown man, bred to civil liberty in a society which has learnt to make nature its instrument, there is no self-enjoyment in the mere consciousness of freedom as exemption from external control, no sense of an object in which he can satisfy himself having been obtained.

Still, just as the demand for and attainment of freedom from external control is the expression of that same self-seeking principle from which the quest for such an object proceeds, so 'freedom' is the natural term by which the man describes such an object to himself,—describes to himself the state in which he shall have realised his ideal of himself, shall be at one with the law which he recognises as that which he ought to obey, shall have become all that he has it in him to be, and so fulfil the law of his being or 'live according to nature.' Just as the consciousness of an unattainable ideal, of a law recognised as having authority but with which one's will conflicts, of wants

and impulses which interfere with the fulfilment of
one's possibilities, is a consciousness of impeded en-
ergy, a consciousness of oneself as for ever thwarted
and held back, so the forecast of deliverance from
these conditions is as naturally said to be a forecast of
'freedom' as of 'peace' or 'blessedness.' Nor is it
merely to a select few, and as an expression for a
deliverance really (as it would seem) unattainable
under the conditions of any life that we know, but
regarded by saints as secured for them in another
world, and by philosophers as the completion of a
process which is eternally complete in God, that 'freedom' commends itself. To any popular audience interested in any work of self-improvement (e.g. to a
temperance-meeting seeking to break the bondage to
liquor), it is as an effort to attain freedom that such
work can be most effectively presented. It is easy to
tell such people that the term is being misapplied;
that they are quite 'free' as it is, because every one can
do as he likes so long as he does not prevent another
from doing so; that in any sense in which there is such
a thing as 'free will,' to get drunk is as much an act of
free will as anything else. Still the feeling of oppression, which always goes along with the consciousness
of unfulfilled possibilities, will always give meaning to
the representation of the effort after any kind of self-
improvement as a demand for 'freedom.' [12]

[12] The remaining sections (§§19-25) deal with problems related to the second point (b) raised at the end of §1. They
include the notion of a 'higher self,' the distinction between
'reason' and 'will,' the idea of moral progress as a progressive
reconciliation between will and reason, and an analysis of the
elements of moral progress in terms of (i) 'conventional morality,' (ii) 'reflective morality,' and (iii) their synthesis. Many
of these topics are treated also in *The Principles of Political
Obligation,* Section A and passim.

THE PRINCIPLES
OF POLITICAL OBLIGATION [1]

A. THE GROUNDS
OF POLITICAL OBLIGATION. [§§1-31]

1. The subject of this course of lectures is the principles of political obligation; and that term is intended to include the obligation of the subject towards the sovereign, the obligation of the citizen towards the state, and the obligation of individuals to each other as enforced by a political superior. My purpose is to consider the moral function or object served by law, or by the system of rights and obligations which the state enforces, and in so doing to discover the true ground or justification for obedience to law. My plan will be (1) to state in outline what I consider the true function of law to be, this being at the same time the true ground of our moral duty to obey the law; and throughout I distinguish moral duty from legal obligation; (2) to examine the chief doctrines of political obligation that have been current in modern Europe, and by criticising them to bring out more clearly the main points of a truer doctrine; (3) to consider in detail the chief rights and obligations enforced in civilised states, inquiring what is their justification, and

[1] Lectures delivered in the University of Oxford, 1879-80; arranged for publication by R. L. Nettleship. The text here is taken from Green's *Works*, Vol. II, pages 335ff.

what is the ground for respecting them on the principle stated.[2]

2. In previous lectures[3] I have explained what I
understand moral goodness to be, and how it is possible that there should be such a thing; in other words
what are the conditions on the part of reason and
will which are implied in our being able to conceive
moral goodness as an object to be aimed at, and to
give some partial reality to the conception. Our results on this question may be briefly stated as follows.

The highest moral goodness we found was an attribute of character, in so far as it issued in acts done
for the sake of their goodness, not for the sake of any
pleasure or any satisfaction of desire which they bring
to the agent. But it is impossible that an action
should be done for the sake of its goodness, unless it
has been previously contemplated as good for some
other reason than that which consists in its being done
for the sake of its goodness. It must have been done,
or conceived as possible to be done, and have been accounted good, irrespectively of the being done from
this which we ultimately come to regard as the highest motive. In other words, a prior morality, founded
upon interests which are other than the pure interest
in being good, and governed by rules of conduct
relative to a standard of goodness other than that
which makes it depend on this interest, is the condition of there coming to be a character governed by
interest in an ideal of goodness. Otherwise this ideal
would be an empty one; it would be impossible to

[2] Green's plan corresponds to the lettered Sections roughly as
follows: Division (1)–primarily Section A, but also Section
G; Division (2)–Sections B, C, D, E, and most of F; Division
(3)–Sections H, I, K, L, M, N, O, P, and the latter parts of
Section F. There is no Section J.

[3] That is, the lectures on the 'Metaphysic of Ethics.' (See
Prolegomena to Ethics, as well as "The Senses of 'Freedom.'")

say what the good actions were, that were to be done for the sake of their goodness; and the interest in this ideal would be impossible, since it would be an interest without an object.

3. When, however, morality of the latter kind has come to be recognised as the highest or the only true morality, the prior morality needs to be criticised from the point of view thus gained. Those interests, other than the interest in being good, which form the motives on the part of the individual on which it rests, will not indeed be rejected as of no moral value; for no one can suppose that without them, or except as regulating them, the pure interest in being good could determine conduct at all. But they will be estimated according to their value as leading up to, or as capable of becoming elements in, a character in which this interest is the governing principle. Again, those rules of conduct, according to which the terms right and wrong, good and bad, are commonly applied, and which, as was just now said, are relative to a standard certainly not founded on the conception of the good as consisting in the character described, are not indeed to be rejected; for without them there would be nothing to define the duties which the highest character is prepared to do for their own sake. But they have to be revised according to a method which inquires into their rationale or justification, as conditions of approximation to the highest character.

4. Such a criticism of moral interests—of the general motives which determine moral conduct and regulate such moral approbation or disapprobation as is not based on a strict theory of moral good—may be called by the name of 'a theory of moral sentiments.' The criticism of recognised rules of conduct will fall under two heads, according as these rules are embodied in positive law (law of which the observance

is enforced on the individual by a political superior),
or only form part of the 'law of opinion' (part of what
the individual feels to be expected of him by some
person or persons to whose expectations he ought to
conform).

5. Moral interests are so greatly dependent on generally recognised rules of conduct that the criticism of
the latter should come first. The law of opinion,
again, in so many ways presupposes a social fabric
supported by 'positive' law, that we can only fairly take
account of it when we have considered the moral value
and justifiability of the fabric so supported. I propose
therefore to begin our inquiry into the detail of goodness—into the particular kinds of conduct which the
man wishing to do good for the sake of its goodness
is entitled to count good—by considering what is of
permanent moral value in the institutions of civil life,
as established in Europe; in what way they have contributed and contribute to the possibility of morality
in the higher sense of the term, and are justified or
have a moral claim upon our loyal conformity, in consequence.

6. The condition of a moral life is the possession
of will and reason. Will is the capacity in a man of
being determined to action by the idea of a possible
satisfaction of himself. An act of will is an action so
determined. A state of will is the capacity as determined by the particular objects in which the man
seeks self-satisfaction; and it becomes a character in
so far as the self-satisfaction is habitually sought in
objects of a particular kind. Practical reason is the
capacity in a man of conceiving the perfection of his
nature as an object to be attained by action. All moral
ideas have their origin in reason, i.e. in the idea of a
possible self-perfection to be attained by the moral
agent. This does not mean that the moral agent in

every stage of his progress could state this idea to himself in an abstract form, any more than in every stage in the acquisition of knowledge about nature a man can state to himself in an abstract form the conception of the unity of nature, which yet throughout conditions the acquisition of his knowledge. Ideas do not first come into existence, or begin to operate, upon the formation of an abstract expression for them. This expression is only arrived at upon analysis of a concrete experience, which they have rendered possible. Thus we only learn to express the idea of self-perfection in that abstract form upon an analysis of an experience of self-improvement which we have ourselves gone through, and which must have been gone through by those with whom we are connected by the possession of language and an organisation of life, however elementary: but the same analysis shows that the same idea must have been at work to make such experience possible. In this idea all particular moral ideas—all ideas of particular forms of conduct as estimable—originate, though an abstract expression for the latter is arrived at much sooner than such an expression for the idea in which they originate. They arise, as the individual's conception of the society on the well-being of which his own depends, and of the constituents of that well-being, becomes wider and fuller; and they are embodied in the laws, institutions, and social expectation, which make conventional morality. This embodiment, again, constitutes the moral progress of mankind. This progress, however, is only a *moral* progress in so far as it tends to bring about the harmony of will and reason, in the only form in which it can really exist, viz. in the characters of persons. And this result is actually achieved, in so far as upon habits disciplined by conformity to conventional morality there supervenes an intelligent interest in some of the objects contributory to human perfection, which that conventional morality subserves, and in so far as that interest becomes the dominant interest of the character.

7. The value then of the institutions of civil life lies in their operation as giving reality to these capacities of will and reason, and enabling them to be really exercised. In their general effect, apart from particular aberrations, they render it possible for a man to be freely determined by the idea of a possible satisfaction of himself, instead of being driven this way and that by external forces, and thus they give reality to the capacity called will: and they enable him to realise his reason, i.e. his idea of self-perfection, by acting as a member of a social organisation in which each contributes to the better-being of all the rest. So far as they do in fact thus operate they are morally justified, and may be said to correspond to the 'law of nature,' the *jus naturæ*, according to the only sense in which that phrase can be intelligibly used.

8. There has been much controversy as to what the *jus naturæ* ('Naturrecht') really is, or whether there is such a thing at all. And the controversy, when it comes to be dealt with in English, is further embarrassed by the fact that we have no one term to represent the full meaning of 'jus' or 'Recht,' as a system of correlative rights and obligations, actually enforced or that should be enforced by law.[4] But the essential questions are: (1) whether we are entitled to distinguish the rights and obligations which are anywhere actually enforced by law from rights and obligations which really exist though not enforced; and (2), if we are entitled to do so, what is to be our

---

[4] The Latin *jus* and the German *Recht* (as well as the French *droit*) have the two-fold meaning of 'right' and 'law.' *Jus naturæ* or *Naturrecht:* Natural Law/Right.

criterion of rights and obligations which are really valid, in distinction from those that are actually enforced.

9. No one would seriously maintain that the system of rights and obligations, as it is anywhere enforced by law,—the 'jus' or 'Recht' of any nation—is all that it ought to be. Even Hobbes holds that a law, though it cannot be unjust, may be pernicious. But there has been much objection to the admission of *natural* rights and obligations. At any rate the phrase is liable to misinterpretation. It may be taken to imply that rights and obligations can exist in a 'state of nature' —a state in which every individual is free to do as he likes—; that legal rights and obligations derive their authority from a voluntary act by which individuals contracted themselves out of this state; and that the individual retains from the state of nature certain rights with which no legal obligations ought to conflict. Such a doctrine is generally admitted to be untenable; but it does not follow from this that there is not a true and important sense in which natural rights and obligations exist,—the same sense as that in which duties may be said to exist though unfulfilled. There is a system of rights and obligations which *should be* maintained by law, whether it is so or not, and which may properly be called 'natural'; not in the sense in which the term 'natural' would imply that such a system ever did exist or could exist independently of force exercised by society over individuals, but 'natural' because necessary to the end which it is the vocation of human society to realise.

10. The 'jus naturæ,' thus understood, is at once distinguished from the sphere of moral duty, and relative to it. It is distinguished from it because admitting of enforcement by law. Moral duties do not admit of being so enforced. The question sometimes

put, whether moral duties should be enforced by law,
is really an unmeaning one; for they simply cannot
be enforced. They are duties to act, it is true, and
an act can be enforced: but they are duties to act
from certain dispositions and with certain motives,
and these cannot be enforced. Nay, the enforcement
of an outward act, the moral character of which depends on a certain motive and disposition, may often
contribute to render that motive and disposition impossible: and from this fact arises a limitation to the
proper province of law in enforcing acts, which will
have to be further considered below. When obligations then are spoken of in this connection, as part of
the 'jus naturæ' correlative to rights, they must always
be understood not as moral duties, not as relative to
states of will, but as relative to outward acts, of which
the performance or omission can and should be enforced. There is a moral duty to discharge such
obligations, and to do so in a certain spirit, but the
obligation is such as that with which law has to do
or may have to do, is relative to an outward act
merely, and does not amount to a moral duty. There
is a moral duty in regard to obligations, but there
can be no obligation in regard to moral duties. Thus
the 'jus naturæ'—the system of rights and obligations,
as it should become no less than as it actually is maintained—is distinct from morality in the proper sense.
But it is relative to it. This is implied in saying that
there is a moral duty in regard to actual obligations,
as well as in speaking of the system of rights and
obligations as it should become. If such language is
justifiable, there must be a moral ground both for
conforming to, and for seeking to develope and improve, established 'Recht'; a moral ground which can
only lie in the moral end served by that established
system.

11. Thus we begin the ethical criticism of law with two principles:—(1) that nothing but external acts can be matter of 'obligation' (in the restricted sense); and (2) that, in regard to that which can be made matter of obligation, the question what should be made matter of obligation—the question how far rights and obligations, as actually established by law, correspond to the true 'jus naturæ'—must be considered with reference to the moral end, as serving which alone law and the obligations imposed by law have their value.[5]

12. Before proceeding, some remarks have to be made as to what is implied in these principles. Does the law, or is it possible that it should, confine its view to external acts? What exactly is meant by an external act? In the case of obligations which I am legally punishable for disregarding, the law, in deciding whether punishment is or is not due, takes account of much beside the external act; and this implies that much beside external action is involved in legal obligation. In the case where the person or property of another is damaged by me, the law does not inquire merely whether the act of damage was done, and done by means of my bodily members, but whether it was done intentionally; and if not done with the direct intention of inflicting the damage, whether the damage arose in a manner that might have been foreseen out of something which I did intend to do: whether, again, if it was done quite accidentally the accident was due to culpable negligence. This, however, does not show that the law can enforce or prevent anything but external action, but only that it is *action* which it seeks to enforce or prevent, for without intention there is no action. We

[5] Green's note quotes extensively from definitions of 'Recht' in treatises on *Naturrecht* by Ulrici and Trendelenburg.

talk indeed of a man acting against his will, but if
this means acting against intention it is what it is impossible to do. What I call an act done against my
will is either (1) an act done by someone else using
my body, through superior force, as a means: in which
case there is an act, but it is not mine (e.g. if another
uses my hand to pull the trigger of a gun by which
someone is shot); or (2) a natural event in which my
limbs are affected in a certain way which causes certain results to another person (e.g. if the rolling of
a ship throws me against another person who is thus
thrown into the water); or (3) an act which I do under
the influence of some strong inducement (e.g. the fear
of death), but which is contrary to some strong wish.
In this case the act is mine, but mine because I intend
it; because it is not against my will as = intention.
In saying, then, that the proper, because the only
possible, function of law is to enforce the performance of or abstinence from external actions, it is implied that its function is to produce or prevent certain
intentions, for without intention on the part of someone there is no act.

13. But if an act necessarily includes intention,
what is the nature of the restriction implied in calling
it external? An external action is a determination of
will as exhibited in certain motions of the bodily members which produce certain effects in the material
world; not a determination of the will as arising from
certain motives and a certain disposition. All that
the law can do is to enjoin or forbid determinations
of will as exhibited in such motions, &c. It does indeed present a motive, for it enforces its injunctions
and prohibitions primarily by fear, by its threat of
certain consequences if its commands are disobeyed.
This enforcement is not an exercise of physical force
in the strict sense, for in this sense no force can pro-

duce an action, since it cannot produce a determination of will; and the only way in which the law or its
administrators employ such force is not in the production but in the prevention of action (as when a
criminal is locked up or the police prevent mischievous persons from assaulting us or breaking into our
houses). But though, in enforcing its commands by
threats, the law is presenting a motive, and thus, according to our distinction, affecting action on its inner
side, it does this solely for the sake of the external
act. It does not regard the relation of the act to the
motive fear as of any intrinsic importance. If the
action is performed without this motive ever coming
into play under the influence of what the moralist
counts higher motives, the purpose of the law is
equally satisfied. Indeed, it is always understood
that its purpose is most thoroughly served when the
threat of pains and penalties has ceased to be necessary, and the obligations correlative to the relations
of individuals and of societies are fulfilled from other
motives. Its business is to maintain certain conditions of life—to see that certain actions are done
which are necessary to the maintenance of those conditions, others omitted which would interfere with
them. It has nothing to do with the motive of the
actions or omissions, on which, however, the moral
value of them depends.

14. It appears, then, that legal obligations—obligations which can possibly form the subject of positive
law—can only be obligations to do or abstain from
certain acts, not duties of acting from certain motives,
or with a certain disposition. It is not a question
whether the law should or should not oblige to anything but performance of outward acts. It simply
cannot oblige to anything else, because the only means
at its command for obtaining the fulfilment of obli-

gations are (1) threats of pain and offers of reward,
by means of which it is possible indeed to secure the
general performance of certain acts, but not their
performance from the motive even of fear of the pain
threatened or hope of the reward offered, much less
from any higher motive; (2) the employment of
physical force, (*a*) in restraining men disposed to
violate obligations, (*b*) in forcibly applying the labour
or the property of those who violate obligations to
make good the breach, so far as is possible; (as, e.g.,
when the magistrate forestalls part of a man's wages
to provide for a wife whom he has deserted, or when
the property of a debtor is seized for the benefit of
his creditors).

15. Only outward acts, then, *can* be matter of legal
obligation; but what sort of outward acts *should* be
matter of legal obligation? The answer to this question arises out of the above consideration of the means
which law employs to obtain the fulfilment of obligations, combined with the view of law as relative to
a moral end, i.e. the formation of a society of persons,
acting from a certain disposition, from interest in the
society as such. Those acts only should be matter
of legal injunction or prohibition of which the performance or omission, irrespectively of the motive
from which it proceeds, is so necessary to the existence of a society in which the moral end stated can
be realised, that it is better for them to be done or
omitted from that unworthy motive which consists
in fear or hope of legal consequences than not to be
done at all.

16. We distinguish, then, the system of rights actually maintained and obligations actually enforced
by legal sanctions ('Recht' or 'jus') from the system
of relations and obligations which *should be* maintained by such sanctions ('Naturrecht'); and we hold

that those actions or omissions should be made obligations which, when made obligations, serve a certain moral end; that this end is the ground or justification or rationale of legal obligation; and that thus we obtain a general rule, of both positive and negative application, in regard to the proper matter or content of legal obligation. For since the end consists in action proceeding from a certain disposition, and since action done from apprehension of legal consequences does not proceed from that disposition, no action should be enjoined or prohibited by law of which the injunction or prohibition interferes with actions proceeding from that disposition, and every action should be so enjoined of which the performance is found to produce conditions favourable to action proceeding from that disposition, and of which the legal injunction does not interfere with such action.

17. Does this general rule give any real guidance in the difficulties which practically arise in regard to the province of law—as to what should be required by law, and what left to the inclination of individuals? What cases are there or have there been of enactments which on this principle we can pronounce wrong? Have attempts ever been made by law to enforce acts as virtuous which lose their virtue when done under fear of legal penalties? It would be difficult, no doubt, to find instances of attempts to enforce by law actions of which we should say that the value lies in the disposition from which they are done, actions, e.g. of disinterested kindness, because the clear conception of virtue as depending not on outward results, but on disposition, is but slowly arrived at, and has never been reflected in law. But without any strictly moral object at all, laws have been made which check the development of the moral disposition. This has been done (a) by legal requirements of reli-

gious observance and profession of belief, which have tended to vitiate the religious source of morality; (*b*) by prohibitions and restraints, unnecessary, or which have ceased to be necessary, for maintaining the social conditions of the moral life, and which interfere with the growth of self-reliance, with the formation of a manly conscience and sense of moral dignity,—in short, with the moral autonomy which is the condition of the highest goodness; (*c*) by legal institutions which take away the occasion for the exercise of certain moral virtues (e.g. the Poor-law[6] which takes away the occasion for the exercise of parental forethought, filial reverence, and neighbourly kindness).

18. Laws of this kind have often been objected to on the strength of a one-sided view of the function of laws; the view, viz., that its only business is to prevent interference with the liberty of the individual. And this view has gained undue favour on account of the real reforms to which it has led. The laws which it has helped to get rid of were really mischievous, but mischievous for further reasons than those conceived of by the supporters of this theory. Having done its work, the theory now tends to become obstructive, because in fact advancing civilisation brings with it more and more interference with the liberty of the individual to do as he likes, and this theory affords a reason for resisting all positive reforms, all reforms which involve an action of the state in the way of promoting conditions favourable to moral life. It is one thing to say that the state in promoting these conditions must take care not to defeat its true end by narrowing the region within which the spontaneity

[6] *The Poor Law:* legislation stemming from Tudor times, providing for public relief for the indigent; amended in 1834 in such a way as to discourage people from seeking public relief. Green's apparent objection should be taken together with the next paragraph (§18).

and disinterestedness of true morality can have play;
another thing to say that it has no moral end to serve
at all, and that it goes beyond its province when it
seeks to do more than secure the individual from
violent interference by other individuals. The true
ground of objection to 'paternal government' is not
that it violates the 'laissez faire' principle and conceives that its office is to make people good, to promote morality, but that it rests on a misconception
of morality. The real function of government being
to maintain conditions of life in which morality shall
be possible, and morality consisting in the disinterested performance of self-imposed duties, 'paternal
government' does its best to make it impossible by
narrowing the room for the self-imposition of duties
and for the play of disinterested motives.

19. The question before us, then, is, In what ways
and how far do the main obligations enforced and
rights maintained by law in all civilised societies contribute to the moral end described; viz. to establish
those conditions of life in which a true, i.e. a disinterested or unselfish morality shall be possible? The
answer to this question will be a theory of the 'jus
naturæ'; i.e. it will explain how far positive law is
what it should be, and what is the ground of the duty
to obey it; in other words, of political obligation.
There are two things from which such a theory must
be distinguished. (1) It is not an inquiry into the
process by which actual law came to be what it is;
nor (2) is it an inquiry how far actual law corresponds
to and is derived from the exercise of certain original
or natural rights. (1) It is not the former, because
the process by which the law of any nation and the
law in which civilised nations agree has come to be
what it is, has not been determined by reference to
that end to which we hold that law ought to be di-

rected and by reference to which we criticise it.
That is to say, the process has not been determined
by any such conscious reference on the part of the
agents in the process. No doubt a desire for social
good as distinct from private pleasure, for what is
good on the whole as distinct from what is good for
the moment, has been a necessary condition of it; but
(*a*), as an agent in the development of law, this has
not reached the form of a conception of moral good
according to that definition of it by which the value
of law is to be estimated; and (*b*) in bringing law to
its present state it has been indistinguishably blended
with purely selfish passions and with the simple struggle for existence.

20. (2) A true theory of 'jus naturæ,' a rationale of
law or ideal of what it should be, is not to be had by
inquiring how far actual law corresponds to, and is
derived from, the exercise of certain original or natural
rights, if that is taken to mean that we know, or can
ascertain, what rights are natural on grounds distinct
from those on which we determine what laws are
justifiable, and that then we can proceed to ascertain
what laws are justifiable by deduction from such
rights. 'Natural rights,' so far as there are such
things, are themselves relative to the moral end to
which perfect law is relative. A law is not good because it enforces 'natural rights,' but because it contributes to the realisation of a certain end. We only
discover what rights are natural by considering what
powers must be secured to a man in order to the
attainment of this end. These powers a perfect law
will secure to their full extent. Thus the consideration of what rights are 'natural' (in the only legitimate
sense) and the consideration what laws are justifiable
form one and the same process, each presupposing a
conception of the moral vocation of man.

21. The doctrine here asserted, that all rights are relative to moral ends or duties, must not be confused with the ordinary statement that every right implies a duty, or that rights and duties are correlative. This of course is true in the sense that possession of a right by any person both implies an obligation on the part of someone else, and is conditional upon the recognition of certain obligations on the part of the person possessing it. But what is meant is something different, viz. that the claim or right of the individual to have certain powers secured to him by society, and the counter-claim of society to exercise certain powers over the individual, alike rest on the fact that these powers are necessary to the fulfilment of man's vocation as a moral being, to an effectual self-devotion to the work of developing the perfect character in himself and others.

22. This, however, is not the ground on which the claim in question has generally been asserted. Apart from the utilitarian theory, which first began to be applied politically by Hume, the ordinary way of justifying the civil rights of individuals (i.e. the powers secured to them by law as against each other), as well as the rights of the state against individuals (i.e. the powers which, with the general approval of society, it exercises against them), has been to deduce them from certain supposed prior rights, called natural rights.[7] In the exercise of these natural rights, it has been supposed, men with a view to their general interest established political society. From that establishment is derived both the system of rights and obligations maintained by law as between man and man, and the right of the state to the submission of its subjects. If the question, then, is raised, why I ought to

[7] The 'natural rights' theory sketched here corresponds roughly to the political theory of Locke.

respect the legal rights of my neighbours, to pay
taxes, or have my children vaccinated, serve in the
army if the state requires it, and generally submit to
the law, the answer according to this theory will be
that if I fail to do so, I shall directly or indirectly be
violating the natural rights of other men; directly in
those cases where the legal rights of my neighbours
are also natural rights, as they very well may be (e.g.
rights of liberty or personal safety); indirectly where
this is not the case, because, although the rights of
the state itself are not natural, and many rights exercised by individuals would not only not be secured
but would not exist at all but for legal enactment,
yet the state itself results from a covenant which
originally, in the exercise of their natural rights, men
made with each other, and to which all born under
the state and sharing the advantages derived from it
must be considered parties. There is a natural right,
therefore, on the part of each member of a state to
have this compact observed, with a corresponding
obligation to observe it; and this natural right of all
is violated by any individual who refuses to obey the
law of the state or to respect the rights, not in themselves natural, which the state confers on individuals.

23. This, on the whole, was the form in which the
ground of political obligation, the justification of established rights, was presented throughout the seventeenth century, and in the eighteenth till the rise of
the 'utilitarian' theory of obligation. Special adapta-
tions of it were made by Hobbes and others. In
Hobbes, perhaps (of whom more later), may be found
an effort to fit an anticipation of the utilitarian theory
of political obligation into the received theory which
traced political obligation, by means of the supposition of a primitive contract, to an origin in natural
right. But in him as much as anyone the language

and framework of the theory of compact is retained,
even if an alien doctrine may be read between the
lines. Of the utilitarian theory of political obligation
more shall be said later. It may be presented in a
form in which it would scarcely be distinguishable
from the doctrine just now stated, the doctrine, viz.,
that the ground of political obligation, the reason why
certain powers should be recognised as belonging to
the state and certain other powers as secured by the
state to individuals, lies in the fact that these powers
are necessary to the fulfilment of man's vocation as a
moral being, to an effectual self-devotion to the work
of developing the perfect character in himself and
others. Utilitarianism proper, however, recognises no
vocation of man but the attainment of pleasure and
avoidance of pain. The only reason why civil rights
should be respected—the only justification of them—
according to it, would be that more pleasure is attained or pain avoided by the general respect for
them; the ground of our consciousness that we ought
to respect them, in other words their ultimate sanction, is the fear of what the consequences would be if
we did not. This theory and that which I deem true
have one negative point in common. They do not
seek the ground of actual rights in a prior natural
right, but in an end to which the maintenance of the
rights contributes. They avoid the mistake of iden-
tifying the inquiry into the ultimate justifiability of
actual rights with the question whether there is a
prior right to the possession of them. The right to
the possession of them, if properly so called, would
not be a mere power, but a power recognised by a
society as one which should exist. This recognition
of a power, in some way or other, as that which should
be, is always necessary to render it a right. Therefore when we had shown that the rights exercised in

political society were derived from prior 'natural'
rights, a question would still remain as to the ground
of those natural rights. We should have to ask why
certain powers were recognised as powers which
should be exercised, and thus became these natural
rights.

24. Thus, though it may be possible and useful to
show how the more seemingly artificial rights are
derived from rights more simple and elementary, how
the rights established by law in a political society are
derived from rights that may be called natural, not
in the sense of being prior to society, but in the sense
of being prior to the existence of a society governed
by written law or a recognised sovereign, still such
derivation is no justification of them. It is no answer
to the question why they should be respected; because this question remains to be asked in regard to
the most primitive rights themselves. Political or
civil rights, then, are not to be explained by derivation from natural rights, but in regard to both political
and natural rights, in any sense in which there can be
truly said to be natural rights, the question has to be
asked, how it is that certain powers are recognised
by men in their intercourse with each other as powers
that should be exercised, or of which the possible
exercise should be secured.

25. I have tried to show in lectures on morals that
the conception expressed by the 'should be' is not
identical with the conception of a right possessed by
some man or men, but one from which the latter conception is derived. It is, or implies on the part of
whoever is capable of it, the conception of an ideal,
unattained condition of himself, as an absolute end.
Without this conception the recognition of a power
as a right would be impossible. A power on the part
of anyone is so recognised by others, as one which

should be exercised, when these others regard it as in some way a means to that ideal good of themselves which they alike conceive: and the possessor of the power comes to regard it as a right through consciousness of its being thus recognised as contributory to a good in which he too is interested. No one therefore can have a right except (1) as a member of a society, and (2) of a society in which some common good is recognised by the members of the society as their own ideal good, as that which should be for each of them. The capacity for being determined by a good so recognised is what constitutes personality in the ethical sense; and for this reason there is truth in saying that only among persons, in the ethical sense, can there come to be rights; (which is quite compatible with the fact that the logical disentanglement of the conception of rights precedes that of the conception of the legal person; and that the conception of the moral person, in its abstract and logical form, is not arrived at till after that of the legal person).

Conversely, everyone capable of being determined by the conception of a common good as his own ideal good, as that which unconditionally should be (of being in that sense an end to himself), in other words, every moral person, is capable of rights; i.e. of bearing his part in a society in which the free exercise of his powers is secured to each member through the recognition by each of the others as entitled to the same freedom with himself. To say that he is capable of rights, is to say that he ought to have them, in that sense of 'ought' in which it expresses the relation of man to an end conceived as absolutely good, to an end which, whether desired or no, is conceived as intrinsically desirable. The moral capacity implies a consciousness on the part of the subject of the capacity that its realisation is an end desirable in itself, and rights are the condition of realising it. Only through the possession of rights can the power of the individual freely to make a common good his own have reality given to it. Rights are what may be called the negative realisation of this power. That is, they realise it in the sense of providing for its free exercise, of securing the treatment of one man by another as equally free with himself, but they do not realise it positively, because their possession does not imply that in any active way the individual makes a common good his own. The possession of them, however, is the condition of this positive realisation of the moral capacity, and they ought to be possessed because this end (in the sense explained) ought to be attained.

26. Hence on the part of every person ('person' in the moral sense explained) the claim, more or less articulate and reflected on, to rights on his own part is co-ordinate with his recognition of rights on the part of others. The capacity to conceive a common good as one's own, and to regulate the exercise of one's powers by reference to a good which others recognise, carries with it the consciousness that powers should be so exercised; which means that there should be rights, that powers should be regulated by mutual recognition. There ought to be rights, because the moral personality,—the capacity on the part of an individual for making a common good his own,— ought to be developed; and it is developed through rights; i.e. through the recognition by members of a society of powers in each other contributory to a common good, and the regulation of those powers by that recognition.

27. In saying that only among 'persons' can there come to be rights, and that every 'person' should have rights, I have been careful to explain that I use 'per-

son' in the moral, not merely in the legal, sense. In dealing, then, with such phrases as 'jura personarum'[8] and 'personal rights,' we must keep in view the difference between the legal and ethical sense of the proposition that all rights are personal, or subsist as between persons. In the legal sense, so far as it is true,—and it is so only if 'person' is used in the sense of Roman law,—it is an identical proposition. A person means a subject of rights and nothing more. Legal personality is derived from the possession of right, not *vice versa*. Like other identical propositions, its use is to bring out and emphasise in the predicate what is included in the understood connotation of the subject; to remind us that when we speak of rights we imply the existence of parties, in English phraseology, capable of suing and being sued. In the ethical sense, it means that rights are derived from the possession of personality as = a rational will (i.e. the capacity which man possesses of being determined to action by the conception of such a perfection of his being as involves the perfection of a society in which he lives), in the sense (*a*) that only among beings possessed of rational will can there come to be rights, (*b*) that they fulfil their idea, or are justifiable, or such rights as should be rights, only as contributing to the realisation of a rational will. It is important to bear this distinction in mind in order that the proposition in its ethical sense, which can stand on its own merits, may not derive apparent confirmation from a juristic truism.

28. The moral idea of personality is constantly tending to affect the legal conception of the relation between rights and persons. Thus the 'jura personarum,' which properly = either rights arising out of 'status,' or rights which not only (like all rights)

---

[8] *Jura personarum:* rights of persons, personal rights.

reside in someone having a legal status and are available against others having a legal status, but are exercised over, or in respect of, someone possessed of such status (e.g. a wife or a servant), come to be understood as rights derived from the human personality or belonging to man as man. It is with some such meaning that English writers on law speak of rights to life and liberty as personal rights. The expression might seem pleonastic, since no right can exist except as belonging to a person in the legal sense. They do not use the phrase either pleonastically or in the sense of the Roman lawyers' 'jura personarum' above, but in the sense that these rights are immediately derived from, or necessarily attach to, the human personality in whatever that personality is supposed to consist. There is no doubt, however, that historically the conception of the moral person, in any abstract form, is not arrived at till after that of the legal person has been thus disentangled and formulated; and further that the abstract conception of the legal person, as the sustainer of rights, is not arrived at till long after rights have been actually recognised and established. But the disentanglement or abstract formulation of the conception of moral personality is quite a different thing from the action of the consciousness in which personality consists.

29. The capacity, then, on the part of the individual of conceiving a good as the same for himself and others, and of being determined to action by that conception, is the foundation of rights; and rights are the condition of that capacity being realised. No right is justifiable or should be a right except on the ground that directly or indirectly it serves this purpose. Conversely every power should be a right, i.e. society should secure to the individual every power, that is

necessary for realising this capacity. Claims to such
powers as are directly necessary to a man's acting as
a moral person at all—acting under the conception
of a good as the same for self and others—may be
called in a special sense personal rights (though they
will include more than Stephen[9] includes under that
designation); they may also be called, if we avoid
misconceptions connected with these terms, 'innate'
or 'natural' rights. They are thus distinguished from
others which are (1) only indirectly necessary to the
end stated, or (2) are so only under special conditions of society; as well as from claims which rest
merely on legal enactment and might cease to be enforced without any violation of the 'jus naturæ.'

30. The objection to calling them 'innate' or 'natural,' when once it is admitted on the one side that
rights are not arbitrary creations of law or custom
but that there are certain powers which ought to be
secured as rights, on the other hand that there are no
rights antecedent to society, none that men brought
with them into a society which they contracted to
form, is mainly one of words. They are 'innate' or
'natural' in the same sense in which according to
Aristotle the state is natural; not in the sense that they
actually exist when a man is born and that they have
actually existed as long as the human race, but that
they arise out of, and are necessary for the fulfilment
of, a moral capacity without which a man would not
be a man. There cannot be innate rights in any
other sense than that in which there are innate duties,
of which, however, much less has been heard. Because a group of beings are capable each of conceiv-

---

[9] Henry John *Stephen* (1787-1864), author of the standard
work, *New Commentaries on the Laws of England* (London,
1841-45 and many subsequent editions).

ing an absolute good of himself and of conceiving it to be good for himself as identical with, and because identical with, the good of the rest of the group, there arises for each a consciousness that the common good should be the object of action, i.e. a duty, and a claim in each to a power of action that shall be at once secured and regulated by the consciousness of a common good on the part of the rest, i.e. a right. There is no ground for saying that the right arises out of a primary human capacity, and is thus 'innate,' which does not apply equally to the duty.

31. The dissociation of innate rights from innate duties has gone along with the delusion that such rights existed apart from society. Men were supposed to have existed in a state of nature, which was not a state of society, but in which certain rights attached to them as individuals, and then to have formed societies by contract or covenant. Society having been formed, certain other rights arose through positive enactment; but none of these, it was held, could interfere with the natural rights which belonged to men antecedently to the social contract or survived it.

Such a theory can only be stated by an application to an imaginary state of things, prior to the formation of societies as regulated by custom or law, of terms that have no meaning except in relation to such societies. 'Natural right,' as = right in a state of nature which is not a state of society, is a contradiction. There can be no right without a consciousness of common interest on the part of members of a society. Without this there might be certain powers on the part of individuals, but no recognition of these powers by others as powers of which they allow the exercise, nor any claim to such recognition; and without this recognition or claim to recognition there can be no right.

[Green now turns to the second part of his program and undertakes "to examine the chief doctrines of political obligation that have been current in modern Europe, and by criticizing them to bring out more clearly the main points of a truer doctrine." (See above, §1.) The sub-divisions of this examination are as follows:

    B. Spinoza (§§32-41)
    C. Hobbes (§§42-50)
    D. Locke (§§51-63)
    E. Rousseau (§§64-79)
    F. Sovereignty and the General Will: Rousseau and
       Austin (§§80-112).]

G. WILL, NOT FORCE, IS THE BASIS OF THE STATE. [§§113-136]

113. Looking back on the political theories which we have discussed, we may see that they all start with putting the question to be dealt with in the same way, and that their errors are very much due to the way in which they put it. They make no inquiry into the development of society and of man through society. They take no account of other forms of community than that regulated by a supreme coercive power, either in the way of investigating their historical origin and connection, or of considering the ideas and states of mind which they imply or which render them possible. They leave out of sight the process by which men have been clothed with rights and duties, and with senses of right and duty, which are neither natural nor derived from a sovereign power. They look only to the supreme coercive power on the one side and to individuals, to whom natural rights are ascribed, on the other, and ask what is the nature and origin of the right of that supreme coercive power

as against these natural rights of individuals. The question so put can only be answered by some device for representing the individuals governed as consenting parties to the exercise of government over them. This they no doubt are so long as the government is exercised in a way corresponding to their several wishes; but, so long as this is the case, there is no interference with their 'natural liberty' to do as they like. It is only when this liberty is interfered with, that any occasion arises for an explanation of the compatibility of the sovereign's right with the natural right of the individual; and it is just then that the explanation by the supposition that the right of the sovereign is founded on consent, fails. But the need of the fictitious explanation[10] arises from a wrong way of putting the question; the power which regulates our conduct in political society is conceived in too abstract a way on the one side, and on the other are set over against it, as the subjects which it controls, individuals invested with all the moral attributes and rights of humanity. But in truth it is only as members of a society, as recognising common interests and objects, that individuals come to have these attributes and rights; and the power, which in a political society they have to obey, is derived from the development and systematisation of those institutions for the regulation of a common life without which they would have no rights at all.

114. To ask why I am to submit to the power of the state, is to ask why I am to allow my life to be regulated by that complex of institutions without which I literally should not have a life to call my own, nor should be able to ask for a justification of what I am called on to do. For that I may have a life

---

[10] *Fictitious explanation:* the idea of Social Contract.

which I can call my own, I must not only be conscious of myself and of ends which I present to myself as mine; I must be able to reckon on a certain freedom of action and acquisition for the attainment of those ends, and this can only be secured through common recognition of this freedom on the part of each other by members of a society, as being for a common good. . . .

120. These considerations[11] may remind us how far removed from any foundation in their own will the requirements of the modern state must seem to be to most of those who have to submit to them. It is true that the necessity which the state lays upon the individual is for the most part one to which he is so accustomed that he no longer kicks against it; but what is it, we may ask, but an external necessity, which he no more lays on himself than he does the weight of the atmosphere or the pressure of summer heat and winter frosts, that compels the ordinary citizen to pay rates and taxes, to serve in the army, to abstain from walking over the squire's fields, snaring his hares, or fishing in preserved streams, to pay rent, to respect those artificial rights of property which only the possessors of them have any obvious interest in maintaining, or even (if he is one of the 'proletariate') to keep his hands off the superfluous wealth of his neighbour, when he has none of his own to lose? Granted that there are good reasons of social expediency for maintaining institutions which thus compel the individual to actions and forbearances that are none of his willing, is it not abusing words to speak

[11] In §119 Green had remarked upon (among other things) the difficulty of achieving "active and direct participation by the citizens" in the politics of the modern state, given its vast size compared with the Greek *polis*.

of them as founded on a conception of general good?
A conception does not float in the air. It must be
somebody's conception. Whose conception, then, of
general good is it that these institutions represent?
Not that of most of the people who conform to them,
for they do so because they are made to, or have come
to do so habitually from having been long made to;
(i.e. from being frightened at the consequences of
not conforming, not consequences which follow from
not conforming in the ordinary course of nature, but
consequences which the state inflicts, artificial consequences). But when a man is said to obey an authority from interest in a common good, some other
good is meant than that which consists in escaping
the punishment which the authority would inflict on
disobedience. Is then the conception of common
good which is alleged a conception of it on the part
of those who founded or who maintain the institutions
in question? But is it not certain that private interests have been the main agents in establishing, and
are still in maintaining, at any rate all the more artificial rights of property? Have not our modern states,
again, in nearly every case been founded on conquest,
and are not the actual institutions of government in
great measure the direct result of such conquest, or,
where revolutions have intervened, of violence which
has been as little governed by any conception of general good? Supposing that philosophers can find ex-
quisite reasons for considering the institutions and
requirements which have resulted from all this self-
seeking and violence to be contributory to the common good of those who have to submit to them, is it
not trifling to speak of them as founded on or representing a conception of this good, when no such conception has influenced those who established, maintain, or submit to them? And is it not seriously mis-

leading, when the requirements of the state have so largely arisen out of force directed by selfish motives, and when the motive to obedience to those requirements is determined by fear, to speak of them as having a common source with the morality of which it is admitted that the essence is to be disinterested and spontaneous?

121. If we would meet these objections fairly, certain admissions must be made. The idea of a common good which the state fulfils has never been the sole influence actuating those who have been agents in the historical process by which states have come to be formed; and even so far as it has actuated them, it has been only as conceived in some very imperfect form that it has done so. This is equally true of those who contribute to the formation and maintenance of states rather as agents, and of those who do so rather as patients. No one could pretend that even the most thoughtful and dispassionate publicist is capable of the idea of the good served by the state to which he belongs, in all its fulness. He apprehends it only in some of its bearings; but it is as a common good that he apprehends it, i.e. not as a good for himself or for this man or that more than another, but for all members equally in virtue of their relation to each other and their common nature. The idea which the ordinary citizen has of the common good served by the state is much more limited in content. Very likely he does not think of it at all in connection with anything that the term 'state' represents to him. But he has a clear understanding of certain interests and rights common to himself with his neighbours, if only such as consist in getting his wages paid at the end of the week, in getting his money's worth at the shop, in the inviolability of his own person and that of his wife. Habitually and instinctively, i.e. without ask-

ing the reason why, he regards the claim which in these respects he makes for himself as conditional upon his recognising a like claim in others, and thus as in the proper sense a right—a claim of which the essence lies in its being common to himself with others. Without this instinctive recognition he is one of the 'dangerous classes,' virtually outlawed by himself. With it, though he have no reverence for the 'state' under that name, no sense of an interest shared with others in maintaining it, he has the needful elementary conception of a common good maintained by law. It is the fault of the state if this conception fails to make him a loyal subject, if not an intelligent patriot. It is a sign that the state is not a true state; that it is not fulfilling its primary function of maintaining law equally in the interest of all, but is being administered in the interest of classes; whence it follows that the obedience which, if not rendered willingly, the state compels the citizen to render, is not one that he feels any spontaneous interest in rendering, because it does not present itself to him as the condition of the maintenance of those rights and interests, common to himself with his neighbours, which he understands.

122. But if the law which regulates private relations and its administration are so equally applied to all, that all who are capable of a common interest are prompted by that interest to conform to the law, the result is still only the loyal subject as distinct from the intelligent patriot, i.e. as distinct from the man who so appreciates the good which in common with others he derives from the state—from the nation organised in the form of a self-governing community to which he belongs—as to have a passion for serving it, whether in the way of defending it from external attack, or developing it from within. The citizens of

the Roman empire were loyal subjects; the admirable maintenance of private rights made them that; but they were not intelligent patriots, and chiefly because they were not, the empire fell. That active interest in the service of the state, which makes patriotism in the better sense, can hardly arise while the individual's relation to the state is that of a passive recipient of protection in the exercise of his rights of person and property. While this is the case, he will give the state no thanks for the protection which he will come to take as a matter of course, and will only be conscious of it when it descends upon him with some unusual demand for service or payment, and then he will be conscious of it in the way of resentment. If he is to have a higher feeling of political duty, he must take part in the work of the state. He must have a share, direct or indirect, by himself acting as a member or by voting for the members of supreme or provincial assemblies, in making and maintaining the laws which he obeys. Only thus will he learn to regard the work of the state as a whole, and to transfer to the whole the interest which otherwise his particular experience would lead him to feel only in that part of its work that goes to the maintenance of his own and his neighbour's rights.

124. But, it will be said, we are here again falling back on our unproved assumption that the state is an institution for the promotion of a common good. This granted, it is not difficult to make out that in most men at any rate there is a sufficient interest in some form of social well-being, sufficient understanding of the community between their own well-being and that of their neighbours, to make them loyal to such an institution. But the question is, whether the promotion of a common good, at any rate in any sense ap-

preciable by the multitude, is any necessary characteristic of a state. It is admitted that the outward visible sign of a state is the presence of a supreme or independent coercive power, to which habitual obedience is rendered by a certain multitude of people,[12] and that this power may often be exercised in a manner apparently detrimental to the general well-being. It may be the case, as we have tried to show that it is, that a power which is in the main so exercised, and is generally felt to be so, is not likely long to maintain its supremacy; but this does not show that a state cannot exist without the promotion of the common good of its subjects, or that (in any intelligible way) the promotion of such good belongs to the idea of a state. A short-lived state is not therefore not a state, and if it were, it is rather the active interference with the subject's well-being, than a failure to promote it, that is fatal to the long life of a state. How, finally, can the state be said to exist for the sake of an end, or to fulfil an idea, the contemplation of which, it is admitted, has had little to do with the actions which have had most to do with bringing states into existence?

125. The last question is a crucial one, which must be met at the outset. It must be noticed that the ordinary conception of organisation, as we apply it in the interpretation of nature, implies that agents may be instrumental in the attainment of an end or the fulfilment of an idea of which there is no consciousness on the part of the organic agents themselves. If it is true on the one hand that the interpretation of nature by the supposition of ends external

---

[12] This characterization of the state is cast in terms of John Austin's definition of 'sovereignty,' which Green had discussed earlier (Section *F*).

to it, with reference to which its processes are directed, has been discarded, and that its rejection has been the condition of growth in an exact knowledge of nature, on the other hand the recognition of ends immanent in nature, of ideas realised within it, is the basis of a scientific explanation of life. The phænomena of life are not ideal, in the sense in which the ideal is opposed to that which is sensibly verifiable, but they are related to the processes of material change which are their conditions, as ideas or ideal ends which those processes contribute to realise, because, while they determine the processes (while the processes would not be what they are but for relation to them), yet they are *not* those processes, *not* identical with any one or number of them, or all of them together. Life does not reside in any of the organs of life, or in any or all of the processes of material change through which these pass. Analyse or combine these as you will, you do not detect it as the result of the analysis or combination. It is a function or end which they realise according to a plan or idea which determines their existence before they exist and survives their disappearance. If it were held, then, that the state were an organised community in the same sense in which a living body is, of which the members at once contribute to the function called life, and are made what they are by that function, according to an idea of which there is no consciousness on their part, we should only be following the analogy of the established method of interpreting nature.

126. The objection to such a view would be that it represents the state as a purely natural, not at all as a moral, organism. Moral agency is not merely an agency by which an end is attained, or an idea

realised, or a function fulfilled, but an agency determined by an idea on the part of the agent, by his conception of an end or function; and the state would be brought into being and sustained by merely natural, as opposed to moral, agency, unless there were a consciousness of ends—and of ends the same in principle with that served by the state itself—on the part of those by whom it is brought into being, and sustained. I say 'ends the same in principle with that served by the state itself,' because, if the state arose out of the action of men determined, indeed, by the consciousness of ends, but ends wholly heterogeneous to that realised by the state, it would not be a moral institution, would not stand in any moral relation to men. Now among the influences that have operated in the formation of states, a large part, it must be admitted, are simply natural. Such are the influences of climate, of distribution of mountain and plain, land and water, &c., of all physical demarcations and means of communication. But these, it is clear, are only organic to the formation of states so far as, so to speak, they take a character, which does not belong to them as merely natural, from agencies distinctively human.

127. 'Human, if you like,' it may be replied, 'but not moral, if a moral agency implies any reference to a social or human good, to a good which the individual desires because it is good for others, or for mankind, as well as himself. In the earth-hunger of conquering hordes, in the passions of military despots, in the pride or avarice or vindictiveness which moved such men as Louis XI or Henry VIII to override the semi-anarchy of feudalism with a real sovereignty, what is there of reference to such good? Yet if we suppose the influence of such motives as these, together with the natural influences just spoken of, to

be erased from the history of the formation of states, its distinguishing features are gone.'

128. The selfish motives described must not, any more than the natural influences, be regarded in abstraction, if we would understand their true place in the formation of states. The pure desire for social good does not indeed operate in human affairs unalloyed by egotistic motives, but on the other hand what we call egotistic motives do not act without direction from an involuntary reference to social good, —'involuntary' in the sense that it is so much a matter of course that the individual does not distinguish it from his ordinary state of mind. The most conspicuous modern instance of a man who was instrumental in working great and in some ways beneficial changes in the political order of Europe, from what we should be apt to call the most purely selfish motives, is Napoleon. Without pretending to analyse these motives precisely, we may say that a leading one was the passion for glory; but if there is to be truth in the statement that this passion governed Napoleon, it must be qualified by the farther statement that the passion was itself governed by social influences, operative on him, from which it derived its particular direction. With all his egotism, his individuality was so far governed by the action of the national spirit in and upon him, that he could only glorify himself in the greatness of France; and though the national spirit expressed itself in an effort after greatness which was in many ways of a mischievous and delusive kind, yet it again had so much of what may be called the spirit of humanity in it, that it required satisfaction in the belief that it was serving mankind. Hence the aggrandisement of France, in which Napoleon's passion for glory satisfied itself, had to take at least the semblance of a deliverance of oppressed peoples, and in taking

the semblance it to a great extent performed the reality; at any rate in western Germany and northern Italy, wherever the Code Napoléon was introduced.

131. The assertion, then, that an idea of social good is represented by, or realised in, the formation of states, is not to be met by pointing to the selfishness and bad passions of men who have been instrumental in forming them, if there is reason to think that the influences, under the direction of which these passions became thus instrumental, are due to the action of such an idea. And when we speak thus we do not refer to any action of the idea otherwise than in the consciousness of men. It may be legitimate, as we have seen, to consider ideas as existing and acting otherwise, and perhaps, on thinking the matter out, we should find ourselves compelled to regard the idea of social good as a communication to the human consciousness, a consciousness developing itself in time, from an eternally complete consciousness. But here we are considering it as a source of the moral action of men, and therefore necessarily as having its seat in their consciousness, and the proposition advanced is that such an idea is a determining element in the consciousness of the most selfish men who have been instrumental in the formation or maintenance of states; that only through its influence in directing and controlling their actions could they be so instrumental; and that, though its active presence in their consciousness is due to the institutions, the organisation of life, under which they are born and bred, the existence of these institutions is in turn due to the action, under other conditions, of the same idea in the minds of men.

132. It is the necessity of a supreme coercive power to the existence of a state that gives plausibility to the view that the action of merely selfish passions may

lead to the formation of states. They have been motive causes, it would seem, in the processes by which this 'imperium' [13] has been established; as, e.g., the acquisition of military power by a tribal chieftain, the conquest of one tribe by another, the supersession of the independent prerogatives of families by a tyrant which was the antecedent condition of the formation of states in the ancient world, the supersession of feudal prerogatives by the royal authority which served the same purpose in modern Europe. It is not, however, supreme coercive power, simply as such, but supreme coercive power exercised in a certain way and for certain ends, that makes a state; viz. exercised according to law, written or customary, and for the maintenance of rights. The abstract consideration of sovereignty has led to these qualifications being overlooked. Sovereignty = supreme coercive power, indeed, but such power as exercised in and over a state, which means with the qualifications specified; but the mischief of beginning with an inquiry into sovereignty before the idea of a state has been investigated, is that it leads us to adopt this abstract notion of sovereignty, as merely supreme coercive power, and then, when we come to think of the state as distinguished by sovereignty, makes us suppose that supreme coercive power is all that is essential to a state, forgetting that it is rather the state that makes the sovereign, than the sovereign that makes the state. Supposing one man had been master of all the slaves in one of the states of the American Union, there would have been a multitude of men under one supreme coercive power, but the slaves and the master would have formed no state, because there would have been no recognised rights of slave against slave enforced by the master, nor would dealings between master and slaves have been regu-

[13] *Imperium:* dominion, supreme power.

lated by any law. The fact that sovereign power, as
implied in the fact of its supremacy, can alter any
laws, is apt to make us overlook the necessity of conformity to law on the part of the sovereign, if he is
to be the sovereign of a state. A power that altered
laws otherwise than according to law, according to a
constitution, written or unwritten, would be incompatible with the existence of a state, which is a body of
persons, recognised by each other as having rights,
and possessing certain institutions for the maintenance
of those rights. The office of the sovereign, as an institution of such a society, is to protect those rights
from invasion, either from without, from foreign nations, or from within, from members of the society who
cease to behave as such. Its supremacy is the society's
independence of such attacks from without or within.
It is an agency of the society, or the society itself acting for this end. If the power, existing for this end, is
used on the whole otherwise than in conformity either
with a formal constitution or with customs which virtually serve the purpose of a constitution, it is no
longer an institution for the maintenance of rights
and ceases to be the agent of a state. We only count
Russia a state by a sort of courtesy on the supposition
that the power of the Czar, though subject to no con-
stitutional control, is so far exercised in accordance
with a recognised tradition of what the public good
requires as to be on the whole a sustainer of rights.

It is true that, just as in a state, all law being derived from the sovereign, there is a sense in which the
sovereign is not bound by any law, so there is a sense
in which all rights are derived from the sovereign, and
no power which the sovereign refuses to allow can be
a right; but it is only in the sense that, the sovereign
being the state acting in a certain capacity, and the
state being an institution for the more complete and

mined, by the conception of a common good. It is not indeed true that only a state can produce a state, though modern history might seem to favour that notion. As a matter of fact, the formation of modern states through feudalism out of an earlier tribal system has been dependent on ideas derived from the Roman state, if not on institutions actually handed down from it; and the improvement and development of the state-system which has taken place since the French Revolution has been through agencies which all presuppose and are determined by the previous existence of states. But the Greek states, so far as we know, were a first institution of the kind, not a result of propagation from previously existing states. But the action which brought them into being was only effectual for its purpose, because the idea of right, though only in the form of family or tribal right, was already in operation.

H. HAS THE CITIZEN RIGHTS AGAINST THE STATE? [§§137-147]

141. A man may . . . have rights as a member of a family or of human society in any other form, without being a member of a state at all,—rights which remain rights though any particular state or all states refuse to recognise them; and a member of a state, on the ground of that capability of living as a freeman among freemen which is implied in his being a member of a state, has rights as against all other states and their members. These latter rights are in fact during peace recognised by all civilised states. It is the object of 'private international law' to reduce them to a system. But though it follows from this that the state does not create rights, it may be still true to say that the members of a state derive their rights from the

state and have no rights against it. We have already
seen that a right against society, as such, is an im-
possibility; that every right is derived from some social
relation; that a right against any group of associated
men depends on association, as ἴσος καὶ ὅμοιος,[14] with
them and with some other men. Now for the member of a state to say that his rights are derived from
his social relations, and to say that they are derived
from his position as member of a state, are the same
thing. The state is for him the complex of those social
relations out of which rights arise, so far as those
rights have come to be regulated and harmonised according to a general law, which is recognised by a
certain multitude of persons, and which there is sufficient power to secure against violation from without
and from within. The other forms of community
which precede and are independent of the formation
of the state, do not continue to exist outside it, nor yet
are they superseded by it. They are carried on into
it. They become its organic members, supporting its
life and in turn maintained by it in a new harmony
with each other. Thus the citizen's rights, e.g. as a
husband or head of a family or a holder of property,
though such rights, arising out of other social relations
than that of citizen to citizen, existed when as yet
there was no state, are yet to the citizen derived from
the state, from that more highly developed form of
society in which the association of the family and
that of possessors who respect each other's possessions
are included as in a fuller whole; which secures to the
citizen his family rights and his rights as a holder of
property, but under conditions and limitations which
the membership of the fuller whole—the reconciliation
of rights arising out of one sort of social capability
with those arising out of another—renders necessary.

[14] As *isos kai homoios*: as an equal.

Nor can the citizen have any right against the state, in the sense of a right to act otherwise than as a member of some society, the state being for its members the society of societies, the society in which all their claims upon each other are mutually adjusted.

142. But what exactly is meant by the citizen's acting 'as a member of his state'? What does the assertion that he can have no right to act otherwise than as a member of his state amount to? Does it mean that he has no right to disobey the law of the state to which he belongs, whatever that law may be? . . . The only unqualified answer that can be given to it is one that may seem too general to be of any practical use, viz. that so far as the laws anywhere or at any time in force fulfil the idea of a state, there can be no right to disobey them; or, that there can be no right to disobey the law of the state except in the interest of the state; i.e. for the purpose of making the state in respect of its actual laws more completely correspond to what it is in tendency or idea, viz. the reconciler and sustainer of the rights that arise out of the social relations of men. On this principle there can be no right to disobey or evade any particular law on the ground that it interferes with any freedom of action, any right of managing his children or 'doing what he will with his own,' which but for that law the individual would possess. . . .

143. . . . On this principle it would follow, if we regard the state as the sustainer and harmoniser of social relations, that the individual can have no right against the state; that its law must be to him of absolute authority. But in fact, as actual states at best fulfil but partially their ideal function, we cannot apply this rule to practice. The general principle that the citizen must never act otherwise than as a citizen, does not carry with it an obligation under all

conditions to conform to the law of his state, since
those laws may be inconsistent with the true end of
the state as the sustainer and harmonizer of social relations. The assertion, however, by the citizen of any
right which the state does not recognize must be
founded on a reference to an acknowledged social
good. . . .

144. . . . He must be able to point to some public
interest, generally recognized as such, which is involved in the exercise of the power claimed by him
as a right; to show that it is not the general well-
being, even as conceived by his fellow-citizens, but
some special interest of a class that is concerned in
preventing the exercise of the power claimed. . . .
As a general rule, no doubt, even bad laws, laws representing the interests of classes or individuals as opposed to those of the community, should be obeyed.
There can be no right to disobey them, even while
their repeal is urged on the ground that they violate
rights, because the public interest, on which all rights
are founded, is more concerned in the general obedience to law than in the exercise of those powers by
individuals or classes which the objectionable laws
unfairly withhold.[15] . . . On the other hand, there
may be cases in which the public interest—not merely
according to some remote philosopher's view of it, but
according to conceptions which the people are able to
assimilate—is best served by a violation of some actual
law. It is so in regard to slavery when the public

[15] Green had raised the question of the right of disobedience
earlier in his discussion of sovereignty (Section *F*), in the
course of which he said: "*In a country like ours, with a popular government and settled methods of enacting and repealing
laws,* . . . [the citizen] should do all he can by legal means
to get the command [of the "political superior"] cancelled, but
till it is cancelled he should conform to it." (§100; my emphasis.) He then went on to discuss the "duty of resistance"
in "extreme cases" (§§101-112).

conscience has come to recognize a capacity for right
(for exercising powers under the control of a reference
to general well-being) in a body of men to whom legal
rights have hitherto been refused, but when some
powerful class in its own interest resists the alteration
of the law. In such a case the violation of the law
on behalf of the slave is not only not a violation in
the interest of the violator; the general sense of right
on which the general observance of law depends being
represented by it, there is no danger of its making a
breach in the law-abiding habits of the people.[16]

145. 'But this,' it will be said, 'is to assume a condition of things in which the real difficulty of the question disappears. What is to be done when no recognition of the implicit rights of the slave can be elicited
from the public conscience; when the legal prohibitions described are supported by the only conceptions
of general good of which the body of citizens is capable? . . .' [The slave has] rights which the state
neither gives nor can take away, and they amount
to or constitute a right to freedom. . . . The obligation to observe the law, because it is the law, does not
exist for him.

146. It is otherwise with the citizen. The slave has
a claim upon him to be treated in a certain way, the
claim which is properly described as that of a common
humanity. But the state which forbids him so to

[16] Here and in §§145-147 Green draws his illustrations from
statutes supporting slavery in the United States before the Civil
War—laws forbidding the harboring of runaway slaves, etc.
During the Civil War itself, Green had been a strong supporter
of the Union cause, largely on anti-slavery grounds. (See
Works, III, xliii-xliv.) The reader may, if he wishes, experi-
ment with translating Green's examples from the slavery issue
into terms of the struggle over racial equality in the United
States of the 1960's. One wonders how Green would have
applied his principles to the issue agitating Great Britain at
the time of his lectures—the 'land question' and the 'crimes'
of the Irish peasants.

treat the slave has also a claim upon him, a claim which embodies many of the claims that arise out of a common humanity in a form that reconciles them with each other. . . .

147. . . . [U]nder certain conditions the right of helping the slave may be cancelled by the duty of obeying the prohibitory law. It would do so if the violation of law in the interest of the slave were liable to result in general anarchy, not merely in the sense of the dissolution of this or that form of civil combination, but of the disappearance of the conditions under which any civil combination is possible; for such a destruction of the state would mean a general loss of freedom, a general substitution of force for mutual good-will in men's dealings with each other, that would outweigh the evil of any slavery under such limitations and regulations as an organised state imposes on it.

I. PRIVATE RIGHTS.
THE RIGHT TO LIFE AND LIBERTY. [§§148-156]

[In §149 Green cites the classification of rights by H. J. Stephen (see §30, note 9): rights are distinguished as pertaining to individuals as (i) persons,[17] (ii) property-owners,[18] (iii) family members,[19] and (iv) citizens of a state.[20] In contrast to class iv ('public rights'), the other three classes comprise 'private rights,' so that the first title of Section I, 'Private Rights,' refers not only to the topics discussed in Section I (the rights to life and liberty, which are 'personal rights' or 'rights of persons' in the sense of class i), but also to most of the following Sections.]

151. If there are such things as rights at all, then, there must be a right to life and liberty, or, to put it

[17] Discussed in Sections I, K, L, and M.
[18] Discussed in Section N.   [19] Discussed in Section O.
[20] This topic was not reached in the lectures. (Cf. §247.)

more properly, to free life. No distinction can be made between the right to life and the right to liberty, for there can be no right to mere life, no right to life on the part of a being that has not also the right to use the life according to the motions of its own will. What is the foundation of this right? The answer is, capacity on the part of the subject for membership of a society, for determination of the will, and through it of the bodily organisation, by the conception of a well-being as common to self with others. This capacity is the foundation of the right, or the right potentially, which becomes actual through the recognition of the capacity by a society, and through the power which the society in consequence secures to the individual of acting according to the capacity. In principle, or intrinsically, or in respect of that which it has it in itself to become, the right is one that belongs to every man in virtue of his human nature (of the qualities that render him capable of any fellowship with any other men), and is a right as between him and any other men; because, as we have seen, the qualities which enable him to act as a member of any one society having the general well-being of its members for its object (as distinct from any special object requiring special talent for its accomplishment) form a capacity for membership of any other such society; but actually, or as recognised, it only gradually becomes a right of a man, as man, and against all men.

[Green proceeds to sketch the development of the idea of personal rights from familial and tribal society, through the limited citizenship of the ancient *polis*, to "the recognition of rights in the man, as independent of particular citizenship" involved in Roman 'equity,' the Stoic 'law of nature,' and the Christian conception of 'universal brotherhood.' (§§152-153)]

154. . . . We often find, however, that men assimilate a practical idea in respect of one of its implications without doing so in respect of the rest. Thus the idea of the individual's right to free life has been strongly laid hold of in Christendom in what may be called an abstract or negative way, but little notice has been taken of what it involves. . . .

155. On the other hand, it is equally noticeable that there are counter-beliefs which, under conditions, do neutralise it, and that certain other beliefs, which form its proper complement, have very slight hold on the mind of modern Christendom. It is taken for granted that the exigencies of the state in war, whether the war be necessary or not for saving the state from dissolution, absolutely neutralise the right to live. We are little influenced by the idea of the universal brotherhood of men, of mankind as forming one society with a common good, of which the conception may determine the action of its members. In international dealings we are apt to suppose that it can have no place at all. Yet, as has been pointed out, it is the proper correlative of the admission of a right to free life as belonging to man in virtue simply of his human nature. And though this right can only be grounded on the capacity, which belongs to the human nature, for freely fulfilling some function in the social organism, we do very little to give reality to the capacity or to enable it to realise itself. We content ourselves with enacting that no man shall be used by other men as a means against his will, but we leave it to be pretty much a matter of chance whether or no he shall be qualified to fulfil any social function, to contribute anything to the common good, and to do so freely (i.e. under the conception of a common good). The only reason why a man should not be used by other men

simply as a means to their ends, is that he should use himself as a means to an end which is really his and theirs at once.   But while we say that he shall not be used as a means, we often leave him without the chance of using himself for any social end at all.

K. THE RIGHT OF THE STATE OVER THE INDIVIDUAL IN WAR. [§§157-175]

[Green considers here the anomaly that the state, which exists to guarantee rights (including the right to life) can require a man to give his life for his country.   War is morally wrong, though it is often difficult to assess the responsibility for it.   Wars stem from "apparently competing interests" among states, and these in turn arise out of "the deficient [internal] organisation of states" (e.g., rule by a privileged class).   This section closes with "the dream of an international court with authority resting on the consent of independent states," a prospect admittedly "very remote," but nevertheless the logical outcome of man's political development.]

L. THE RIGHT OF THE STATE TO PUNISH. [§§176-206]

[Green considers here the apparent anomaly that the state, in order effectively to guarantee the right to life and liberty to some, may have to deny it to others (i.e., to criminals). A theory of rights requires a theory of punishment for the violation of rights, and Green interprets "punishment according to its proper nature" as three-fold: "retributive" ("the criminal should have his due"), "preventive," and "reformatory."]

M. THE RIGHT OF THE STATE
TO PROMOTE MORALITY. [§§207-210] [21]

207. The right of the individual man as such to free
life is constantly gaining on its negative side more
general recognition. It is the basis of the growing
scrupulosity in regard to punishments which are not
reformatory, which put rights finally out of the reach
of a criminal instead of qualifying him for their re-
newed exercise. But the only rational foundation
for the ascription of this right is the ascription of capacity for free contribution to social good. We treat
this capacity in the man whose crime has given proof
of its having been overcome by anti-social tendencies,
as yet giving him a title to a further chance of its development; on the other hand, we act as if it conferred
no title on its possessors, before a crime has been com-
mitted, to be placed under conditions in which its
realisation would be possible. Is this reasonable?
Yet are not all modern states so acting? Are they not
allowing their ostensible members to grow up under
conditions which render the development of social
capacity practically impossible? Was it not more reasonable, as in the ancient states, to deny the right to
life in the human subject as such, than to admit it
under conditions which prevent the realisation of the
capacity that forms the ground of its admission? . . .
What is the nature and extent of the individual's claim
to be enabled positively to realise that capacity for

[21] This Section treats the last issue raised in §155. The title
of the Section (given by Nettleship) is somewhat misleading:
equally appropriate would have been "The Right of the Individual to the Conditions of a Moral Life."

freely contributing to social good which is the foundation of his right to free life?

208. In dealing with this question, it is important to bear in mind that the capacity we are considering is essentially a free or (what is the same) a moral capacity. It is a capacity, not for action determined by relation to a certain end, but for action determined by a conception of the end to which it is relative. Only thus is it a foundation of rights. The action of an animal or plant may be made contributory to social good, but it is not therefore a foundation of rights on the part of an animal or plant, because they are not affected by the conception of the good to which they contribute. A right is a power of acting for his own ends,—for what he conceives to be his good,—secured to an individual by the community, on the supposition that its exercise contributes to the good of the community. But the exercise of such a power cannot be so contributory, unless the individual, in acting for his own ends, is at least affected by the conception of a good as common to himself with others. The condition of making the animal contributory to human good is that we do not leave him free to determine the exercise of his powers; that we determine them for him; that we use him merely as an instrument; and this means that we do not, because we cannot, endow him with rights. We cannot endow him with rights because there is no conception of a good common to him with us which we can treat as a motive to him to do to us as he would have us do to him. It is not indeed necessary to a capacity for rights, as it is to true moral goodness, that interest in a good conceived as common to himself with others should be a man's dominant motive. It is enough if that which he presents to himself from time to time as his good, and which accordingly determines his action, is so far af-

fected by consideration of the position in which he
stands to others,—of the way in which this or that
possible action of his would affect them, and of what
he would have to expect from them in return,—as to
result habitually, without force or fear of force, in
action not incompatible with conditions necessary to
the pursuit of a common good on the part of others.
In other words, it is the presumption that a man in his
general course of conduct will of his own motion have
respect to the common good, which entitles him to
rights at the hands of the community. The question
of the moral value of the motive which may induce this
respect—whether an unselfish interest in common
good or the wish for personal pleasure and fear of
personal pain—does not come into the account at all.
An agent, indeed, who could only be induced by fear
of death or bodily harm to behave conformably to the
requirements of the community, would not be a subject of rights, because this influence could never be
brought to bear on him so constantly, if he were free
to regulate his own life, as to secure the public safety.
But a man's desire for pleasure to himself and aver-
sion from pain to himself, though dissociated from any
desire for a higher object, for any object that is desired because good for others, may constitute a capacity for rights, if his imagination of pleasure and pain
is so far affected by sympathy with the feeling of
others about him as to make him, independently of
force or fear of punishment, observant of established
rights. In such a case the fear of punishment may be
needed to neutralise anti-social impulses under circumstances of special temptation, but by itself it could
never be a sufficiently uniform motive to qualify a
man, in the absence of more spontaneously social feel-
ings, for the life of a free citizen. The qualification

for such a life is a spontaneous habit of acting with reference to a common good, whether that habit be founded on an imagination of pleasures and pains or on a conception of what ought to be. In either case the habit implies at least an understanding that there is such a thing as a common good, and a regulation of egoistic hopes and fears, if not an inducing of more 'disinterested' motives, in consequence of that understanding.

209. The capacity for rights, then, being a capacity for spontaneous action regulated by a conception of a common good, either so regulated through an interest which flows directly from that conception, or through hopes and fears which are affected by it through more complex channels of habit and association, is a capacity which cannot be generated—which on the contrary is neutralised—by any influences that interfere with the spontaneous action of social interests. Now any direct enforcement of the outward conduct, which ought to flow from social interests, by means of threatened penalties—and a law requiring such conduct necessarily implies penalties for disobedience to it—does interfere with the spontaneous action of those interests, and consequently checks the growth of the capacity which is the condition of the beneficial exercise of rights. For this reason the effectual action of the state, i.e. the community as acting through law, for the promotion of habits of true citizenship, seems necessarily to be confined to the removal of obstacles. Under this head, however, there may and should be included much that most states have hitherto neglected, and much that at first sight may have the appearance of an enforcement of moral duties, e.g. the requirement that parents have their children taught the elementary arts. To educate one's children is no

doubt a moral duty, and it is not one of those duties, like that of paying debts, of which the neglect directly interferes with the rights of someone else. It might seem, therefore, to be a duty with which positive law should have nothing to do, any more than with the duty of striving after a noble life. On the other hand, the neglect of it does tend to prevent the growth of the capacity for beneficially exercising rights on the part of those whose education is neglected, and it is on this account, not as a purely moral duty on the part of a parent, but as the prevention of a hindrance to the capacity for rights on the part of children, that education should be enforced by the state. It may be objected, indeed, that in enforcing it we are departing in regard to the parents from the principle above laid down; that we are interfering with the spontaneous action of social interests, though we are doing so with a view to promoting this spontaneous action in another generation. But the answer to this objection is, that a law of compulsory education, if the preferences, ecclesiastical or otherwise, of those parents who show any practical sense of their responsibility are duly respected, is from the beginning only felt as compulsion by those in whom, so far as this social function is concerned, there is no spontaneity to be interfered with; and that in the second generation, though the law with its penal sanctions still continues, it is not felt as a law, as an enforcement of action by penalties, at all.

210. On the same principle the freedom of contract ought probably to be more restricted in certain directions than is at present the case. The freedom to do as they like on the part of one set of men may involve the ultimate disqualification of many others, or of a succeeding generation, for the exercise of rights. This applies most obviously to such kinds of contract or

raffic as affect the health and housing of the people, he growth of population relatively to the means of ubsistence, and the accumulation or distribution of anded property. In the hurry of removing those estraints on free dealing between man and man, vhich have arisen partly perhaps from some confused dea of maintaining morality, but much more from the ower of class-interests, we have been apt to take too aarrow a view of the range of persons—not one generation merely, but succeeding generations—whose reedom ought to be taken into account, and of he conditions necessary to their freedom ('freedom' here meaning their qualification for the exercise of rights). Hence the massing of population without egard to conditions of health; unrestrained traffic in deleterious commodities; unlimited upgrowth of the class of hired labourers in particular industries which circumstances have suddenly stimulated, without any provision against the danger of an impoverished proletariate in following generations. Meanwhile, under pretence of allowing freedom of bequest and settlement, a system has grown up which prevents the andlords of each generation from being free either in he government of their families or in the disposal of heir land, and aggravates the tendency to crowd into towns, as well as the difficulties of providing healthy house-room, by keeping land in a few hands. It would be out of place here to consider in detail the remedies for these evils, or to discuss the question how far it is well to trust to the initiative of the state or of individuals in dealing with them. It is enough to point out the directions in which the state may remove obstacles to the realisation of the capacity for beneficial exercise of rights, without defeating its own object by vitiating the spontaneous character of that capacity.

N. RIGHTS OF PROPERTY. [§§211-232] [22]

211. We have now considered the ground of the
right to free life, and what is the justification, if any,
for the apparent disregard of that right, (a) in war,
(b) in the infliction of punishment. We have also
dealt with the question of the general office of the
state in regard to the development of that capacity
in individuals which is the foundation of the right,
pointing out on the one hand the necessary limitation
of its office in this respect, on the other hand the directions in which it may remove obstacles to that development. We have next to consider the rationale of
the rights of property.

In discussions on the 'origin of property' two questions are apt to be mixed up which, though connected,
ought to be kept distinct. One is the question how
men have come to appropriate; the other the question
how the idea of right has come to be associated with
their appropriations. As the term 'property' not only
implies a permanent possession of something, or a
possession which can only be given up with the good
will of the possessor, but also a possession recognised
as a right, an inquiry into the origin of property must
involve both these questions, but it is not the less important that the distinction between them should be
observed. Each of them again has both its analytical
and its historical side. In regard to the first question
it is important to learn all that can be learnt as to the
kind of things that were first, and afterwards at suc-

---

[22] I have dropped Nettleship's title for this Section ("The
Right of the State in Regard to Property"), in view of the fact
that Green's discussion is concerned with the individual's right
to acquire, use, and bequeath property, as much as with the
state's right to regulate it.

cessive periods, appropriated; as to the mode in which, and the sort of persons or societies by whom, they were appropriated. This is an historical inquiry. But it cannot take the place of a metaphysical or psychological [23] analysis of the conditions on the part of the appropriating subject implied in the fact that he does such a thing as appropriate. So, too, in regard to the second question, it is important to investigate historically the forms in which the right of men in their appropriations has been recognised; the parties, whether individuals or societies, to whom the right has been allowed; and the sort of objects, capable of appropriation, to which it has been considered to extend. But neither can these inquiries help us to understand, in the absence of a metaphysical or moral analysis, either what is implied in the ascription of a right to certain appropriations, or why there should be a right to them.

212. We have then two questions, as above stated, each requiring two different methods of treatment. But neither have the questions themselves, nor the different methods of dealing with them, been duly distinguished.

It is owing to confusion between them that the right of property in things has been supposed to originate in the first occupancy of them. This supposition, in truth, merely disguises the identical proposition that in order to [be] property there must to begin with have been some appropriation. The truism that there could

---

[23] *Psychological:* Green speaks here in the classical tradition that regarded psychology as a branch of philosophy. What he has in mind is perhaps closer to what has become known as 'phenomenology' (the analysis of typical structures of experience) than to what we are apt to think of today as 'psychology' (which is more concerned to reduce mental states and actions either to biological stimuli or to unconscious motivations).

be no property in anything which had not been at some time and in some manner appropriated, tells us nothing as to how or why the property in it, as a right, came to be recognised, or why that right should be recognised. But owing to the confusion between the origin of appropriation and the origin of property as a right, an identical proposition as to the beginning of appropriation seemed to be an instructive statement as to the basis of the rights of property. Of late, in a revulsion from theories founded on identical propositions, 'historical' inquiries into the 'origin of property' have come into vogue. The right method of dealing with the question has been taken to lie in an investigation of the earliest forms in which property has existed. But such investigation, however valuable in itself, leaves untouched the questions, (1) what it is in the nature of men that makes it possible for them, and moves them, to appropriate; (2) why it is that they conceive of themselves and each other as having a right in their appropriations; (3) on what ground this conception is treated as a moral authority,—as one that should be acted on.

213. (1) Appropriation is an expression of will; of the individual's effort to give reality to a conception of his own good; of his consciousness of a possible self-satisfaction as an object to be attained. It is different from mere provision to supply a future want. . . . [Acts of appropriation] are not merely a passing employment of such materials as can be laid hands on to satisfy this or that want, present or future, felt or imagined, but reflect the consciousness of a subject which distinguishes itself from its wants; which presents itself to itself as still there and demanding satisfaction when this or that want, or any number of wants, have been satisfied; which thus not merely uses

a thing to fill a want, and in so doing at once destroys the thing and for the time removes the want, but says to itself, 'This shall be mine to do as I like with, to satisfy my wants and express my emotions as they arise.'

214. [(2)] One condition of the existence of property, then, is appropriation, and that implies the conception of himself on the part of the appropriator as a permanent subject for whose use, as instruments of satisfaction and expression, he takes and fashions certain external things, certain things external to his bodily members. These things, so taken and fashioned, cease to be external as they were before. They become a sort of extension of the man's organs, the constant apparatus through which he gives reality to his ideas and wishes. But another condition must be fulfilled in order to constitute property, even of the most simple and primitive sort. This is the recognition by others of a man's appropriations as something which they will treat as his, not theirs, and the guarantee to him of his appropriations by means of that recognition. What then is the ground of the recognition? The writers of the seventeenth and eighteenth centuries, who discussed the basis of the rights of property, took it for granted, and in so doing begged the question. Grotius makes the right of property rest on contract, but clearly until there is a recognised 'meum' and 'tuum' [24] there can be no contract. Contract presupposes property.[25] . . . Hobbes is so far more logical that he does not derive property from contract, but treats property and 'the validity of covenants' as co-ordinately dependent on the existence of a sover-

[24] *Meum* and *tuum:* mine and thine.
[25] Green's note quotes Hugo Grotius' *De jure belli et paci* (1625), Book II, Ch. ii, §1, §§4-5. Grotius (1583-1645) was a Dutch jurist and political theorist.

eign power of compulsion.[26]   But his account of this, as of all other forms of right, is open to the objection . . . that if the sovereign power is merely a strongest force it cannot be a source of rights; and that if it is other than this, if it is a representative and maintainer of rights, its existence presupposes rights, which remain to be accounted for. . . .

215. Locke[27] treats property—fairly enough so long as only its simplest forms are in question—as derived from labour. By the same law of nature and reason by which a man has 'a property in his own person,' 'the labour of his body and the work of his hand are properly his' too. Now that the right to free life, which we have already dwelt on, carries with it a certain right to property, to a certain permanent apparatus beyond the bodily organs, for the maintenance and expression of that life, is quite true. But apart from the difficulty of tracing some kinds of property, in which men are in fact held to have a right, to the labour of anyone, even of someone from whom it has been derived by inheritance or bequest (a difficulty to be considered presently), to say that it is a 'law of nature and reason' that a man should have a property in the work of his hands is no more than saying that that on which a man has impressed his labour is recognised by others as something which should be his, just as he himself is recognised by them as one that should be his own master. The ground of the recognition is the same in both cases, and it is Locke's merit to have pointed this out; but what the ground is he does not consider, shelving the question by appealing to a law of nature and reason.

[26] Green's note quotes Hobbes' *Leviathan*, Part II, Chs. xv xviii.
[27] Green cites Locke's *Second Treatise of Civil Government* Ch. v.

216. [(3)] The ground of the right to free life, the reason why a man is secured in the free exercise of his powers through recognition of that exercise by others as something that should be, lay, as we saw, in the conception on the part of everyone who concedes the right to others and to whom it is conceded, of an identity of good for himself and others. It is only as within a society, as a relation between its members, though the society be that of all men, that there can be such a thing as a right; and the right to free life rests on the common will of the society, in the sense that each member of the society within which the right subsists contributes to satisfy the others in seeking to satisfy himself, and that each is aware that the other does so; whence there results a common interest in the free play of the powers of all. And just as the recognised interest of a society constitutes for each member of it the right to free life, just as it makes each conceive of such life on the part of himself and his neighbour as what should be, and thus forms the basis of a restraining custom which secures it for each, so it constitutes the right to the instruments of such life, making each regard the possession of them by the other as for the common good, and thus through the medium first of custom, then of law, securing them to each.

217. Thus the doctrine that the foundation of the right of property lies in the will, that property is 'realised will,' is true enough if we attach a certain meaning to 'will'; if we understand by it, not the momentary spring of any and every spontaneous action, but a constant principle, operative in all men qualified for any form of society, however frequently overborne by passing impulses, in virtue of which each seeks to give reality to the conception of a well-being which he necessarily regards as common to himself with others. A will of this kind explains at once the effort to ap-

propriate, and the restraint placed on each in his appropriations by a customary recognition of the interest which each has in the success of the like effort on
the part of the other members of a society with which
he shares a common well-being. This customary
recognition, founded on a moral or rational will, requires indeed to be represented by some adequate
force before it can result in a real maintenance of the
rights of property. The wild beast in man will not
otherwise yield obedience to the rational will. And
from the operation of this compulsive force, very imperfectly controlled by the moral tendencies which
need its co-operation,—in other words from the historical incidents of conquest and government,—there
result many characteristics of the institution of property, as it actually exists, which cannot be derived
from the spiritual principle which we have assigned as
its foundation. Still, without that principle it could
not have come into existence, nor would it have any
moral justification at all.

218. It accords with the account given of this principle that the right of property, like every other form
of right, should first appear within societies founded
on kinship, these being naturally the societies within
which the restraining conception of a common well-
being is first operative. We are apt indeed to think
of the state of things in which the members of a family
or clan hold land and stock in common, as the an-
tithesis of one in which rights of property exist. In
truth it is the earliest stage of their existence, because
the most primitive form of society in which the fruit
of his labour is secured to the individual by the society, under the influence of the conception of a common well-being. The characteristic of primitive communities is not the absence of distinction between
'meum' and 'tuum,' without which no society of intel-

ligent as opposed to instinctive agents would be possible at all, but the common possession of certain materials, in particular land, on which labour may be expended. It is the same common interest which prevents the separate appropriation of these materials, and which secures the individual in the enjoyment and use of that which his labour can extract from them.

219. From the moral point of view, however, the clan-system is defective, because under it the restraint imposed upon the individual by his membership of a society is not, and has not the opportunity of becoming, a self-imposed restraint, a free obedience, to which, though the alternative course is left open to him, the individual submits, because he conceives it as his true good. The area within which he can shape his own circumstances is not sufficient to allow of the opposite possibilities of right and wrong being presented to him, and thus of his learning to love right for its own sake. And the other side of this moral tutelage of the individual, this withholding from him of the opportunity of being freely determined by recognition of his moral relations, is the confinement of those relations themselves, which under the clan-system have no actual existence except as between members of the same clan. A necessary condition at once of the growth of a free morality, i.e. a certain behaviour of men determined by an understanding of moral relations and by the value which they set on them as understood, and of the conception of those relations as relations between all men, is that free play should be given to every man's powers of appropriation. Moral freedom is not the same thing as a control over the outward circumstances and appliances of life. It is the end to which such control is a generally necessary means, and which gives it its value. In order to obtain this control, men must cease to be limited in

their activities by the customs of the clan. The range of their appropriations must be extended; they must include more of the permanent material on which labour may be expended, and not merely the passing products of labour spent on unappropriated material; and they must be at once secured and controlled in it by the good-will, by the sense of common interest, of a wider society, of a society to which any and every one may belong who will observe its conditions, and not merely those of a particular parentage; in other words by the law, written or unwritten, of a free state.

220. It is too long a business here to attempt an account of the process by which the organisation of rights in the state has superseded that of the clan, and at the same time the restriction of the powers of appropriation implied in the latter has been removed. It is important to observe, however, that this process has by no means contributed unmixedly to the end to which, from the moral point of view, it should have contributed. That end is at once the emancipation of the individual from all restrictions upon the free moral life, and his provision with means for it. But the actual result of the development of rights of property in Europe, as part of its general political development, has so far been a state of things in which all indeed *may* have property, but great numbers in fact cannot have it in that sense in which alone it is of value, viz. as a permanent apparatus for carrying out a plan of life, for expressing ideas of what is beautiful, or giving effect to benevolent wishes. In the eye of the law they have rights of appropriation, but in fact they have not the chance of providing means for a free moral life, of developing and giving reality or expression to a good will, an interest in social well-being. A man who possesses nothing but his powers

of labour and who has to sell these to a capitalist for bare daily maintenance, might as well, in respect of the ethical purposes which the possession of property should serve, be denied rights of property altogether. Is the existence of so many men in this position, and the apparent liability of many more to be brought to it by a general fall of wages, if increase of population goes along with decrease in the productiveness of the earth, a necessary result of the emancipation of the individual and the free play given to powers of appropriation? or is it an evil incident, which may yet be remedied, of that historical process by which the development of the rights of property has been brought about, but in which the agents have for the most part had no moral objects in view at all?

221. Let us first be clear about the points in which the conditions of property, as it actually exists, are at variance with property according to its idea or as it should be. The rationale of property, as we have seen, is that everyone should be secured by society in the power of getting and keeping the means of realising a will, which in possibility is a will directed to social good. Whether anyone's will is actually and positively so directed, does not affect his claim to the power. This power should be secured to the individual irrespectively of the use which he actually makes of it, so long as he does not use it in a way that interferes with the exercise of like power by another, on the ground that its uncontrolled exercise is the condition of attainment by man of that free morality which is his highest good. It is not then a valid objection to the manner in which property is possessed among us, that its holders constantly use it in a way demoralising to themselves and others, any more than such misuse of any other liberties is an objection to securing men in their possession. Only then is property held in a

way inconsistent with its idea, and which should, if possible, be got rid of, when the possession of property by one man interferes with the possession of property by another; when one set of men are secured in the power of getting and keeping the means of realising their will, in such a way that others are practically denied the power. In that case it may truly be said that 'property is theft.'[28] The rationale of property, in short, requires that everyone who will conform to the positive condition of possessing it, viz. labour, and the negative condition, viz. respect for it as possessed by others, should, so far as social arrangements can make him so, be a possessor of property himself, and of such property as will at least enable him to develope a sense of responsibility, as distinct from mere property in the immediate necessaries of life.

222. But then the question arises, whether the rationale of property, as thus stated, is not inconsistent with the unchecked freedom of appropriation, or freedom of appropriation checked only by the requirement that the thing appropriated shall not have previously been appropriated by another. Is the requirement that every honest man should be a proprietor to the extent stated, compatible with any great inequalities of possession? In order to give effect to it, must we not remove those two great sources of the inequality of fortunes, (1) freedom of bequest, and the other arrangements by which the profits of the labour of several generations are accumulated on persons who do not labour at all; (2) freedom of trade, of buying in the cheapest market and selling in the dearest, by which accumulated profits of labour become suddenly multiplied in the hands of a particular proprietor? Now clearly, if an inequality of fortunes, of the

[28] 'Property is theft': a slogan made famous by the French socialist theorist, Pierre Joseph Proudhon (1809-65).

kind which naturally arises from the admission of these
two forms of freedom, necessarily results in the existence of a proletariate, practically excluded from
such ownership as is needed to moralise a man, there
would be a contradiction between our theory of the
right of property and the actual consequence of admitting the right according to the theory; for the theory logically necessitates freedom both in trading and
in the disposition of his property by the owner, so
long as he does not interfere with the like freedom on
the part of others; and in other ways as well its realisation implies inequality.

223. Once admit as the idea of property that nature
should be progressively adapted to the service of man
by a process in which each, while working freely or for
himself, i.e. as determined by a conception of his own
good, at the same time contributes to the social good,
and it will follow that property must be unequal.   If
we leave a man free to realise the conception of a possible well-being, it is impossible to limit the effect
upon him of his desire to provide for his future well-
being, as including that of the persons in whom he is
interested, or the success with which at the prompt-
ing of that desire he turns resources of nature to account. Considered as representing the conquest of
nature by the effort of free and variously gifted individuals, property must be unequal; and no less
must it be so if considered as a means by which individuals fulfil social functions. As we may learn
from Aristotle, those functions are various and the
means required for their fulfilment are various. The
artist and man of letters require different equipment
and apparatus from the tiller of land and the smith.
Either then the various apparatus needed for various
functions must be provided for individuals by society,
which would imply a complete regulation of life in-

compatible with that highest object of human attainment, a free morality; or we must trust for its provision to individual effort, which will imply inequality between the property of different persons.

224. The admission of freedom of trade follows from the same principle. It is a condition of the more complete adaptation of nature to the service of man by the free effort of individuals. 'To buy in the cheapest and sell in the dearest market' is a phrase which may no doubt be used to cover objectionable transactions, in which advantage is taken of the position of sellers who from circumstances are not properly free to make a bargain. It is so employed when the cheapness of buying arises from the presence of labourers who have no alternative but to work for 'starvation wages.' But in itself it merely describes transactions in which commodities are bought where they are of least use and sold where they are of most use. The trader who profits by the transaction is profiting by what is at the same time a contribution to social well-being.

In regard to the freedom which a man should be allowed in disposing of his property by will or gift, the question is not so simple. The same principle which forbids us to limit the degree to which a man may provide for his future, forbids us to limit the degree to which he may provide for his children, these being included in his forecast of his future. It follows that the amount which children may inherit may not rightly be limited; and in this way inequalities of property, and accumulations of it to which possessors have contributed nothing by their own labour, must arise. Of course the possessor of an estate, who has contributed nothing by his own labour to its acquisition, may yet by his labour contribute largely to the social good, and a well-organised state will in various ways elicit

such labour from possessors of inherited wealth.   Nor
will it trust merely to encouraging the voluntary fulfilment of social functions, but will by taxation make
sure of some positive return for the security which
it gives to inherited wealth.   But while the mere per-
mission of inheritance, which seems implied in the per-
mission to a man to provide unlimitedly for his future,
will lead to accumulations of wealth, on the other
hand, if the inheritance is to be equal among all children, and, failing children, is to pass to the next of
kin, the accumulation will be checked. It is not
therefore the right of inheritance, but the right of bequest, that is most likely to lead to accumulation of
wealth, and that has most seriously been questioned
by those who hold that universal ownership is a condition of moral well-being.   Is a proprietor to be allowed to dispose of his property as he likes among his
children (or, if he has none, among others), making
one very rich as compared with the others, or is he to
be checked by a law requiring approximately equal inheritance? [29]

225. As to this, consider that on the same principle
on which we hold that a man should be allowed to
accumulate as he best can for his children, he should
have discretion in distributing among his children.
He should be allowed to accumulate, because in so

[29] Throughout this discussion, the reader should keep in mind
the distinction between (1) the legal requirement of equal
inheritance (as in France); (2) the traditional English system
of primogeniture (whereby the entire estate went to the eldest
son) and power of settlement or entailment (whereby a man
could legally bind his heirs not to break up or sell outside of
the family the estate he bequeathed them); and (3) Green's
own position, which involved the removal of legal sanctions
from primogeniture and settlement, but not (for England, at
any rate) the legal requirement of equal inheritance.   In short,
Green was for 'free trade' in land, which he assumed would
operate to spread ownership more widely.

doing he at once expresses and developes the sense
of family responsibility, which naturally breeds a
recognition of duties in many other directions. But
if the sense of family responsibility is to have free play,
the man must have due control over his family, and
this he can scarcely have if all his children as a matter
of necessity inherit equally, however undutiful or idle
or extravagant they may be. For this reason the true
theory of property would seem to favour freedom of
bequest, at any rate in regard to wealth generally.
There may be special reasons, to be considered presently, for limiting it in regard to land. But as a general rule, the father of a family, if left to himself and
not biassed by any special institutions of his country,
is most likely to make that distribution among his
children which is most for the public good. If family
pride moves him to endow one son more largely than
the rest, in order to maintain the honour of his name,
family affection will keep this tendency within limits
in the interest of the other children, unless the institutions of his country favour the one tendency as against
the other. And this they will do if they maintain great
dignities, e.g. peerages, of which the possession of
large hereditary wealth is virtually the condition, and
if they make it easy, when the other sons have been
impoverished for the sake of endowing the eldest, to
maintain the former at the public expense by means of
appointments in the church or state.

It must be borne in mind, further, that the freedom
of bequest which is to be justified on the above
principles must not be one which limits that freedom
in a subsequent generation. It must therefore be distinguished from the power of settlement allowed by
English law and constantly exercised in dealing with
landed estate; for this power, as exercised by the land-
owning head of a family in one generation, prevents

the succeeding head of the family from being free to make what disposition he thinks best among his children and ties up the succession to the estate to his eldest son.   The practice of settlement in England, in short, as applied to landed estate, cancels the freedom of bequest in the case of most landowners and neutralises all the dispersive tendency of family affection, while it maintains in full force all the accumulative tendency of family pride.   This, however, is no essential incident of a system in which the rights of individual ownership are fully developed, but just the contrary.

226. The question then remains, whether the full development of those rights, as including that of unlimited accumulation of wealth by the individual and of complete freedom of bequest on his part, necessarily carries with it the existence of a proletariate, nominal owners of their powers of labour, but in fact obliged to sell these on such terms that they are owners of nothing beyond what is necessary from day to day for the support of life, and may at any time lose even that, so that, as regards the moral functions of property, they may be held to be not proprietors at all; or whether the existence of such a class is due to causes only accidentally connected with the development of rights of individual property.

We must bear in mind that the increased wealth of one man does not naturally mean the diminished wealth of another.   We must not think of wealth as a given stock of commodities of which a larger share cannot fall to one without taking from the share that falls to another.   The wealth of the world is constantly increasing in proportion as the constant production of new wealth by labour exceeds the constant consumption of what is already produced.   There is no natural limit to its increase except such as arises from the fact that the supply of the food necessary to sustain labour becomes more difficult as more comes to be required owing to the increase in the number of labourers, and from the possible ultimate exhaustion of the raw materials of labour in the world. Therefore in the accumulation of wealth, so far as it arises from the saving by anyone of the products of his labour, from his bequest of this capital to another who farther adds to it by saving some of the profit which the capital yields, as employed in the payment for labour or in trade either by the capitalist himself or someone to whom he lends it, and from the continuation of this process through generations, there is nothing which tends to lessen for anyone else the possibilities of ownership. On the contrary, supposing trade and labour to be free, wealth must be constantly distributed throughout the process in the shape of wages to labourers and of profits to those who mediate in the business of exchange.

227. It is true that the accumulation of capital naturally leads to the employment of large masses of hired labourers. But there is nothing in the nature of the case to keep these labourers in the condition of living from hand to mouth, to exclude them from that education of the sense of responsibility which depends on the possibility of permanent ownership. There is nothing in the fact that their labour is hired in great masses by great capitalists to prevent them from being on a small scale capitalists themselves. In their position they have not indeed the same stimulus to saving, or the same constant opening for the investment of savings, as a man who is αὐτουργός[30]; but their combination in work gives them every opportunity, if they have the needful education and

[30] *Autourgos*: self-employed.

self-discipline, for forming societies for the investment
of savings. In fact, as we know, in the well-paid industries of England the better sort of labourers do
become capitalists, to the extent often of owning their
houses and a good deal of furniture, of having an interest in stores, and of belonging to benefit-societies
through which they make provision for the future. It
is not then to the accumulation of capital, but to the
condition, due to antecedent circumstances uncon-
nected with that accumulation, of the men with whom
the capitalist deals and whose labour he buys on the
cheapest terms, that we must ascribe the multiplica-
tion in recent times of an impoverished and reckless
proletariate.

228. It is difficult to summarise the influences to
which is due the fact that in all the chief seats of
population in Europe the labour-market is constantly
thronged with men who are too badly reared and fed
to be efficient labourers; who for this reason, and from
the competition for employment with each other, have
to sell their labour very cheap; who have thus seldom
the means to save, and whose standard of living and
social expectation is so low that, if they have the opportunity of saving, they do not use it, and keep
bringing children into the world at a rate which perpetuates the evil. It is certain, however, that these
influences have no necessary connection with the
maintenance of the right of individual property and
consequent unlimited accumulation of capital, though
they no doubt are connected with that régime of
force and conquest by which existing governments
have been established,—governments which do not
indeed create the rights of individual property, any
more than other rights, but which serve to maintain
them. It must always be borne in mind that the
appropriation of land by individuals has in most coun-

tries—probably in all where it approaches complete-ness—been originally effected, not by the expenditure of labour or the results of labour on the land, but by force. The original landlords have been conquerors.

229. This has affected the condition of the indus-trial classes in at least two ways: (1) When the ap-plication of accumulated capital to any work in the way of mining or manufacture has created a demand for labour, the supply has been forthcoming from men whose ancestors, if not themselves, were trained in habits of serfdom; men whose life has been one of virtually forced labour, relieved by church-charities or the poor law (which in part took the place of these charities); who were thus in no condition to contract freely for the sale of their labour, and had nothing of that sense of family-responsibility which might have made them insist on having the chance of sav-ing. Landless countrymen, whose ancestors were serfs, are the parents of the proletariate of great towns. (2) Rights have been allowed to landlords, incompatible with the true principle on which rights of property rest, and tending to interfere with the development of the proprietorial capacity in others. The right to freedom in unlimited acquisition of wealth, by means of labour and by means of the sav-ing and successful application of the results of labour, does not imply the right of anyone to do as he likes with those gifts of nature, without which there would be nothing to spend labour upon. The earth is just as much an original natural material necessary to productive industry, as are air, light, and water, but while the latter from the nature of the case cannot be appropriated, the earth can be and has been. The only justification for this appropriation, as for any other, is that it contributes on the whole to social well-being; that the earth as appropriated by indi-

viduals under certain conditions becomes more serviceable to society as a whole, including those who are not proprietors of the soil, than if it were held in common. The justification disappears if these conditions are not observed; and from government having been chiefly in the hands of appropriators of the soil, they have not been duly observed. Landlords have been allowed to 'do what they would with their own,' as if land were merely like so much capital, admitting of indefinite extension. The capital gained by one is not taken from another, but one man cannot acquire more land without others having less; and though a growing reduction in the number of landlords is not necessarily a social evil, if it is compensated by the acquisition of other wealth on the part of those extruded from the soil, it is only not an evil if the landlord is prevented from so using his land as to make it unserviceable to the wants of men (e.g. by turning fertile land into a forest), and from taking liberties with it incompatible with the conditions of general freedom and health; e.g. by clearing out a village and leaving the people to pick up house-room as they can elsewhere (a practice common under the old poor-law, when the distinction between close and open villages grew up), or, on the other hand, by building houses in unhealthy places or of unhealthy structure, by stopping up means of communication, or forbidding the erection of dissenting chapels. In fact the restraints which the public interest requires to be placed on the use of land if individual property in it is to be allowed at all, have been pretty much ignored, while on the other hand, that full development of its resources, which individual ownership would naturally favour, has been interfered with by laws or customs which, in securing estates to certain families, have taken away the interest, and tied the hands, of the nominal owner—the tenant for life—in making the most of his property.

230. Thus the whole history of the ownership of land in Europe has been of a kind to lead to the agglomeration of a proletariate, neither holding nor seeking property, wherever a sudden demand has arisen for labour in mines or manufactures. This at any rate was the case down to the epoch of the French Revolution; and this, which brought to other countries deliverance from feudalism, left England, where feudalism had previously passed into unrestrained landlordism, almost untouched. And while those influences of feudalism and landlordism which tend to throw a shiftless population upon the centres of industry have been left unchecked, nothing till quite lately was done to give such a population a chance of bettering itself, when it had been brought together. Their health, housing, and schooling were unprovided for. They were left to be freely victimised by deleterious employments, foul air, and consequent craving for deleterious drinks. When we consider all this, we shall see the unfairness of laying on capitalism or the free development of individual wealth the blame which is really due to the arbitrary and violent manner in which rights over land have been acquired and exercised, and to the failure of the state to fulfil those functions which under a system of unlimited private ownership are necessary to maintain the conditions of a free life.

231. Whether, when those functions have been more fully recognised and executed, and when the needful control has been established in the public interest over the liberties which landlords may take in the use of their land, it would still be advisable to limit the right of bequest in regard to land, and establish a system of something like equal inheritance,

is a question which cannot be answered on any absolute principle. It depends on circumstances. Probably the question should be answered differently in a country like France or Ireland, where the most important industries are connected directly with the soil, and in one like England where they are not so. The reasons must be cogent which could justify that interference with the control of the parent over his family, which seems to be implied in the limitation of the power of bequeathing land when the parent's wealth lies solely in land, and which arises, be it remembered, in a still more mischievous way from the present English practice of settling estates. But it is important to bear in mind that the question in regard to land stands on a different footing from that in regard to wealth generally, owing to the fact that land is a particular commodity limited in extent, from which alone can be derived the materials necessary to any industry whatever, on which men must find house-room if they are to find it at all, and over which they must pass in communicating with each other, however much water or even air may be used for that purpose. These are indeed not reasons for preventing private property in land or even free bequest of land, but they necessitate a special control over the exercise of rights of property in land, and it remains to be seen whether that control can be sufficiently established in a country where the power of great estates has not first been broken, as in France, by a law of equal inheritance.

232. To the proposal that 'unearned increment' in the value of the soil, as distinct from value produced by expenditure of labour and capital, should be appropriated by the state, though fair enough in itself, the great objection is that the relation between earned and unearned increment is so complicated, that a

system of appropriating the latter to the state could scarcely be established without lessening the stimulus to the individual to make the most of the land, and thus ultimately lessening its serviceableness to society.

O. FAMILY RIGHTS. [§§233-246] [31]

P. RIGHTS AND VIRTUES. [§§247-251] [32]

247. We have now considered in a perfunctory way those rights which are antecedent to the state, which are not derived from it but may exist where a state is not, and which it is the office of the state to maintain. We have inquired what it is in the nature of man that renders him capable of these rights, what are the moral ends to which the rights are relative, and in what form the rights should be realised in order to the attainment of these ends [*sic*]. In order to make the inquiry into rights complete, we ought to go on to examine in the same way the rights which arise out of the establishment of a state, the rights connected with the several functions of government; how these functions come to be necessary, and how

[31] I have substituted this title for Nettleship's ("The Right of the State in Regard to the Family"), since the Section deals with the rights and duties of persons involved in family life (*qua* husband, father, etc.), and not only with the state's regulation of marriage and divorce.

[32] Green has now reached the end of his allotted time without having treated all the topics he had intended—a plight familiar to academics. The main topics not covered are: (1) public or political rights (see §149 and §247), and (2) the 'social virtues' and 'moral sentiments' (see §§247ff.). With these remarks on the virtues, compare *Prolegomena to Ethics,* §§246-290, "The Greek and the Modern Conceptions of Virtue."

they may best be fulfilled with a view to those moral
ends to which the functions of the state are ultimately
relative. According to my project, I should then have
proceeded to consider the social virtues, and the
'moral sentiments' which underlie our particular judgments as to what is good and evil in conduct. All
virtues are really social; or, more properly, the distinction between social and self-regarding virtues is
a false one. Every virtue is self-regarding in the
sense that it is a disposition, or habit of will, directed
to an end which the man presents to himself as his
good; every virtue is social in the sense that unless
the good to which the will is directed is one in which
the well-being of society in some form or other is
involved, the will is not virtuous at all.

248. The virtues are dispositions to exercise positively, in some way contributory to social good, those
powers which, because admitting of being so exercised, society should secure to him; the powers which
a man has a right to possess, which constitute his
rights. It is therefore convenient to arrange the
virtues according to the division of rights. E.g. in
regard to the right of all men to free life, the obligations, strictly so called, correlative to that right having been considered (obligations which are all of a
negative nature, obligations to forbear from meddling
with one's neighbour), we should proceed to consider
the activities by which a society of men really free is
established, or by which some approach is made to
its establishment ('really free,' in the sense of being
enabled to make the most of their capabilities).
These activities will take different forms under different social conditions, but in rough outline they are
those by which men in mutual helpfulness conquer
and adapt nature, and overcome the influences which
would make them victims of chance and accident, of

brute force and animal passion. The virtuous disposition displayed in these activities may have various
names applied to it according to the particular direction in which it is exerted; 'industry,' 'courage,' 'public
spirit.' A particular aspect of it was brought into
relief among the Greeks under the name of ἀνδρεία.[33]
The Greek philosophers already gave an extension to
the meaning of this term beyond that which belonged
to it in popular usage, and we might be tempted further to extend it so as to cover all the forms in which
the habit of will necessary to the maintenance and
furtherance of free society shows itself. The name,
however, does not much matter. It is enough that
there are specific modes of human activity which contribute directly to maintain a shelter for man's wor-
thier energies against disturbance by natural forces
and by the consequences of human fear and lust.
The state of mind which appears in them may properly be treated as a special kind of virtue. It is true
that the principle and the end of all virtues is the
same. They are all determined by relation to social
well-being as their final cause, and they all rest on a
dominant interest in some form or other of that well-
being; but as that interest may take different directions in different persons, as it cannot be equally
developed at once in everyone, it may be said roughly
that a man has one kind of virtue and not others.

249. As the kind of moral duties (in distinction
from those obligations which are correlative to rights)
which relate to the maintenance of free society and
the disposition to fulfil those duties should form a
special object of inquiry, so another special kind
would be those which have to do with the management of property, with the acquisition and expenditure of wealth. To respect the rights of property in

---

[33] *Andreia:* manliness.

others, to fulfil the obligations correlative to those
rights, is one thing; to make a good use of property,
to be justly generous and generously just in giving
and receiving, is another, and that may properly be
treated as a special kind of virtue which appears in
the duly blended prudence, equity, and generosity
of the ideal man of business. Another special kind
will be that which appears in family relations; where
indeed that merely negative observance of right,
which in other relations can be distinguished from
the positive fulfilment of moral duties, becomes unmeaning. As we have seen, there are certain aggra-
vations and perpetuations of wrong from which husband or wife or children can be protected by law,
but the fulfilment of the claims which arise out of
the marriage-tie requires a virtuous will in the active
and positive sense—a will governed by unselfish interests—on the part of those concerned.

250. What is called 'moral sentiment' is merely a
weaker form of that interest in social well-being
which, when wrought into a man's habits and strong
enough to determine action, we call virtue. So far
as this interest is brought into play on the mere survey
of action, and serves merely to determine an approbation or disapprobation, it is called moral sentiment.
The forms of moral sentiment accordingly should be
classified on some principle as forms of virtue, i.e.
with relation to the social functions to which they
correspond.

251. For the convenience of analysis, we may treat
the obligations correlative to rights, obligations which
it is the proper office of law to enforce, apart from
moral duties and from the virtues which are tendencies to fulfil those duties. I am properly *obliged* to
those actions and forbearances which are necessary
to the general freedom, necessary if each is not to

interfere with the realisation of another's will. My
duty is to be interested positively in my neighbour's
well-being. And it is important to understand that,
while the enforcement of obligations is possible, that
of moral duties is impossible. But the establishment
of obligations by law or authoritative custom, and
the gradual recognition of moral duties, have not
been separate processes. They have gone on together in the history of man. The growth of the institutions by which more complete equality of rights
is gradually secured to a wider range of persons,
and of those interests in various forms of social well-
being by which the will is moralised, have been related to each other as the outer and inner side of the
same spiritual development, though at a certain stage
of reflection it comes to be discovered that the agency
of force, by which the rights are maintained, is ineffectual for eliciting the moral interests. The result
of the twofold process has been the creation of the
actual content of morality; the articulation of the
indefinite consciousness that there is something that
should be—a true well-being to be aimed at other
than any pleasure or succession of pleasures—into
the sentiments and interests which form an 'enlightened conscience.' It is thus that when the highest
stage of reflective morality is reached, and upon interests in this or that mode of social good there supervenes an interest in an ideal of goodness, that ideal
has already a definite filling; and the man who pur-
sues duty for duty's sake, who does good for the sake
of being good or in order to realise an idea of perfection, is at no loss to say what in particular his duty
is, or by what particular methods the perfection of
character is to be approached.

BIBLIOGRAPHY

I. GREEN'S WRITINGS

Prolegomena to Ethics, edited by A. C. Bradley (Oxford, 1883 and later). Green's major philosophical work; not included in the *Works* below.

The Works of Thomas Hill Green, edited by R. L. Nettleship (London, 3 vols., 1885-88 and later).
   Vol. I: Philosophical Works contains Green's "Introductions" to Hume's *Treatise,* as well as his articles on Herbert Spencer and G. H. Lewes.
   Vol. II: Philosophical Works contains Green's lectures on Kant, Mill's *Logic,* "The Senses of 'Freedom,' " and *The Principles of Political Obligation.*
   Vol. III: Miscellanies and Memoir includes various essays of which "Christian Dogma" (c. 1864), "The Philosophy of Aristotle" (1866), and "Popular Philosophy in Its Relation to Life" (1868) are particularly important; several review articles on books by British neo-Hegelians; two Lay Sermons on "The Witness of God" and "Faith;" and various lectures on Biblical themes, on the 17th century Puritan Commonwealth, on "Liberal Legislation and Freedom of Contract," and on the condition of English education. Nettleship's "Memoir" (pp. xi-cxli) contains passages from Green's political speeches, in addition to much other material.
Lectures on the Principles of Political Obligation, together with "The Senses of 'Freedom,' " was reprinted from the *Works* as a separate book in 1895 and later.

II. BIOGRAPHICAL

Nettleship's "Memoir" of Green (Green's *Works,* Vol. III) remains standard. Nettleship knew Green intimately, had access to his papers, and solicited recollections of Green from various others who had known him.

James Bryce, *Studies in Contemporary Biography* (London & New York, 1903), "Thomas Hill Green." An earlier version appeared in *The Contemporary Review* (London), May 1882.

Mrs. Humphry Ward's novel, *Robert Elsmere* (London & New York, 1888 and later), gives a free—and adulatory—rendering of Green's character and religious views in the guise of an Oxford Tutor, 'Mr. Grey,' who speaks passages from Green's Lay Sermons. The novel is also dedicated to Green's memory. For Mrs. Ward's comments on the models for her characters, see her Introduction to the Autograph Edition, *The Writings of Mrs. Humphry Ward: Robert Elsmere* (Boston & New York, 1909), Vol. I. Mrs. Ward's personal recollections of Green can be found in *A Writer's Reminiscences* (New York & London, 1918), Vol. I, 176ff.

Melvin Richter, *The Politics of Conscience: T. H. Green and His Times* (London, 1964), contains some additional biographical material drawn from Victorian letters, memoirs, and other sources.

III. ON GREEN'S POLITICAL THEORY

John MacCunn, *Six Radical Thinkers* (London, 1907).

J. H. Muirhead, *The Service of the State: Four Lectures on the Political Teaching of T. H. Green* (London, 1908).

Ernest Barker, *Political Thought in England from Herbert Spencer to the Present Day* (London & New York, 1915).

Yueh Liu Chin, *The Political Theory of Thomas Hill Green* (New York, 1920).

A. D. Lindsay, "T. H. Green and the Idealists," in *The Social and Political Ideas of Some Representative Thinkers of the Victorian Age,* edited by F. J. C. Hearnshaw (London, 1933). Reprinted as an Introduction to the 1941 and later editions of Green's *Lectures on the Principles of Political Obligation.*

H. D. Lewis, "Individualism and Collectivism: A Study of T. H. Green" (*Ethics,* Oct. 1952).

Melvin Richter, "T. H. Green and His Audience: Liberalism as a Surrogate Faith" (*Review of Politics,* Oct. 1956).

IV. ON GREEN'S PHILOSOPHY

W. H. Fairbrother, *The Philosophy of Thomas Hill Green* (London, 1896).

Henry Sidgwick, *Lectures on the Ethics of T. H. Green, Mr. Herbert Spencer, and J. Martineau* (London & New York, 1902).

————, *Lectures on the Philosophy of Kent and Other Philosophical Lectures* (London & New York, 1905), "The Metaphysics of T. H. Green."

W. D. Lamont, *Introduction to Green's Moral Philosophy* (London, 1934).

A. J. M. Milne, *The Social Philosophy of English Idealism* (London, 1962).

V. IN THE TRADITION
OF GREEN'S POLITICAL THEORY

Arnold Toynbee, *Lectures on the Industrial Revolution in England, Popular Addresses, Notes and Other Fragments,* with a memoir by Benjamin Jowett (London, 1884).

Andrew Seth and R. B. Haldane, editors, *Essays in Philosophical Criticism* (London, 1883). See especially the Preface by Edward Caird and the essays by D. G. Ritchie, Henry Jones, and James Bonar.

David G. Ritchie, *The Principles of State Interference* (London, 1891).

———, *Natural Rights* (London & New York, 1895).

Bernard Bosanquet, *The Philosophical Theory of the State* (London & New York, 1899).

Herbert Samuel, *Liberalism: An Attempt to State the Principles and Proposals of Contemporary Liberalism in England,* with an Introduction by the Rt. Hon. H. H. Asquith (London, 1902).

L. T. Hobhouse, *Liberalism* (London & New York, 1911).

Property: Its Duties and Rights, Historically, Philosophically and Religiously Regarded, essays by various writers, with an Introduction by the Bishop of Oxford [Charles Gore] (London, 1913). See especially the essays by Hastings Rashdall and A. D. Lindsay.

Harold J. Laski, *A Grammar of Politics* (London & New Haven, 1925), Chapter 4.

————, *The Decline of Liberalism* (London, 1940).

Guido de Ruggiero, *The History of European Liberalism* (London, 1927).

W. Y. Elliott, *The Pragmatic Revolt in Politics* (New York, 1928).

John Dewey, *Liberalism and Social Action* (New York, 1935).

A. D. Lindsay, *The Modern Democratic State* (London & New York, 1943).

Ernest Barker, *Principles of Social and Political Theory* (Oxford, 1951).

VI. GENERAL BACKGROUND

J. H. Muirhead, *The Platonic Tradition in Anglo-Saxon Philosophy* (London & New York, 1931).

A. V. Dicey, *Lectures on the Relation Between Law and Public Opinion in England During the Nineteenth Century* (London, 1905).

S. MacCoby, editor, *The English Radical Tradition, 1763-1914* (London, 1952).

Adam B. Ulam, *Philosophical Foundations of English Socialism* (Cambridge, Mass., 1951).

David Nicholls, "Positive Liberty: 1880-1914" (*American Political Science Review,* March 1962).